THE EMIRATES
BY THE
FIRST PHOTOGRAPHERS

Water carriers at Al-'Ain Oasis. (R. Codrai c.1950)

THE EMIRATES
BY THE
FIRST PHOTOGRAPHERS

WILLIAM FACEY
AND
GILLIAN GRANT

STACEY INTERNATIONAL   LONDON

The Emirates by the First Photographers
by William Facey and Gillian Grant

This edition published by Stacey International,
128, Kensington Church Street, London W8 4BH

Publisher: David C. Tennant
Editor: Leslie McLoughlin
Art Director: John Fitzmaurice

©The London Centre of Arab Studies, 1996

ISBN 0 905743 91 1

Set by South Bucks Photosetters Limited, Beaconsfield, Buckinghamshire, England

Origination by Spot On Repro Limited, Perivale, Middlesex, England

Printing and binding by Oriental Press, Dubai, UAE

PHOTOGRAPHS

Previous page **The fort at Abu Dhabi in 1954**

This page **Wind-towers at Dubai seen from the landward side. (March 1962)**

Following page **Shindagah seen from Dubai. (March 1958)**

CONTENTS

FOREWORD

PERHAPS only once in a generation is it possible to publish an historic photographic record of a nation. Usually changes are sufficiently slow as to make more frequent publication repetitious. However, the speed of social and economic change in the United Arab Emirates has made it more difficult for the younger generations to maintain a link with aspects and traditions of their cultural heritage. In this progressive Gulf state, the path to modernity has been so rapid that a way of life, familiar to a previous generation, has all but vanished.

It is an awareness of these changes that has motivated us to publish this book. To research and record a former way of life for the benefit of future generations and, at the same time, provide a sometimes nostalgic view of the past for those who made the changes possible.

Captured for all time, through the lens of a camera, this heritage is revealed through a unique collection of photographs, most of which have never been published before. These photographs, accompanied by an authoritative text, span the first sixty years of this century. They tell a remarkable story of a sturdy and determined people, and of a state that has literally grown from the sand.

In the short space of thirty five years, the exploitation of rich oil fields, combined with judicious planning and development, has propelled the United Arab Emirates onto the international stage, to take her place alongside the nations of the world. This leap to modernity was not without its struggles and difficulties, but these seven small shaikhdoms have been blessed with wise and far-sighted leadership.

It is fitting that *The Emirates by the First Photographers* is published in this Jubilee Year. Now, twenty five years after independence, is a good time to look back - to reflect on the past, its tragedies and triumphs, its challenges and achievements. For without knowledge of the past, we have no future.

David C. Tennant
Publisher

The Trucial States: images from the formative years
1900-1965

By 1900 the Gulf had become, in contrast to much of the preceding century, a lively international arena. Ottoman Turkey, France, Germany, Russia, and even a resurgent Persia, each set a challenge, in its different way, to Britain's political and commercial supremacy.

One might therefore have expected the first known photographer of the Emirates, or the Trucial Coast as it was then known, to have been an Englishman, a Frenchman, a German, a Russian, a Turk or even a Persian. It was, however, an American missionary, the Reverend Samuel M. Zwemer who, it seems, must be given the credit for taking the first photographs inside what is today the United Arab Emirates, in 1901.

By Zwemer's time, photography was commonplace in the Middle East, and travellers with cameras and a variety of motives had penetrated other parts of Arabia, notably the Hijaz and the Holy Places of Islam. Closer to the Gulf, photographs of the much-frequented ports of Aden and Muscat, on the steamer route to British India since the opening of the Suez Canal in 1869, were a familiar sight before the end of the 19th century.

There are tantalising hints of still earlier photographic activity in and near the Gulf. Between 1846 and 1848 a French sea-captain, C. Guillain, collected a mass of information on the history, geography and commerce of the East African coast. This was published in about 1856 with a volume of lithographs, some of which were based on *épreuves daguerriennes,* that is, daguerrotypes – the earliest kind of photographic prints. Shortly after Guillain's expedition we hear of another Frenchman, Major H. Ban, who is mentioned, in an April 1857 issue of the magazine *La Lumière,* as having participated in a photographic expedition to the Gulf itself.

"The castle at Abu Thabi" in 1901, by the Rev. Samuel M. Zwemer – probably the first photograph ever taken in Abu Dhabi, and possibly the first on the Trucial Coast, although Zwemer is known to have visited Sharjah in 1900. Zwemer travelled with only one companion and little baggage, and so probably used a small hand camera. Of Abu Dhabi he wrote: "With the exception of a dozen houses and an imposing castle, the whole town is built of date mats and extends along the seashore for nearly two miles."

It is unlikely, in view of Britain's tight watch over the Trucial Coast, that Ban and his crew visited the shaikhdoms. In those days such voyages used to take in Bandar Abbas, Lingah and Bushire (Abu Shahr) on the Persian side, rather than risking the uncertain Arabian shore, before making for Bahrain or Kuwait, and perhaps Muhammarah and Basra on the Shatt al-'Arab. This episode is nonetheless interesting as it came a mere eighteen years after Ban's compatriot, Jacques Mandé Daguerre, had announced the first photographic process to the Académie des Sciences in Paris.

During the intervening period experimenters such as the Englishmen W. H. Fox-Talbot and Frederick Scott-Archer had continued to improve upon the daguerrotype, developing negative-positive processes, using first paper and then glass as the carrier for the light-sensitive salts. The equipment required for all of these early processes was cumbersome and expensive, as well as demanding a great deal of technical expertise. Nevertheless, the new medium attracted increasing numbers of people eager and with the means to acquire the necessary skills. By the time of Major Ban's expedition, several European photographers had begun to visit the Middle East.

The first of these photographers, understandably, attempted to imitate the painter's art, producing picturesque views and detailed architectural studies of ancient and Islamic sites throughout Egypt and the Ottoman Empire. But, as photography gained a wider currency, its more practical uses became apparent, and this carried it beyond the main centres of population to areas as yet unmapped. The Ottoman, Persian and Egyptian armed forces, for example, were quick to realise its value. It was an Egyptian army officer named Muhammad Sadiq who, in 1861, took the earliest known photographs in Arabia, as part of a survey of the routes between the Red Sea port of Wajh and the Holy City of Madinah.

Although the next two decades saw many commercial, professional photographic studios set up in towns and cities throughout the Middle East, the Arabian Peninsula remained untouched by this development. However, the 1870s and 1880s brought notable advances in photographic techniques which would ultimately enable more amateurs to take their own photographs there. The key process was the gelatin dry-plate, first publicised by R.L. Maddox in 1871. His new solution, once set and dried, could be used for some time after preparation, and thus made the commercial manufacture of photographic plates possible. By the 1880s several brands were available, and at the same time many new and smaller cameras began to appear. All of this had obvious advantages for the travelling amateur photographer, such as the explorer or adventurous official or scholar. No longer did cumbersome equipment have to be transported, nor did wet plates have to be prepared on the spot in often difficult conditions, and so cameras could now venture further afield.

In 1885, for example, Samuel Barrett Miles, Britain's Political Agent and Consul at Muscat, was able to take photographs on one of his journeys into the interior of Oman. His ultimate goal was Buraimi, which he had visited in 1875, apparently without a camera. In 1885, being forced to turn back at Dhank, he returned to Muscat via Rustaq, and so just missed the distinction of becoming the first photographer in the territory of the shaikhdoms.

The story of early photography in the Trucial States is closely tied to the history of British involvement there, and the great majority of the early photographers were, inevitably, British – officials, naval men, explorers and, latterly, airmen, soldiers and oil company personnel.

By Miles' time, the Trucial States of Abu Dhabi, Dubai and Sharjah were independent shaikhdoms which, during the course of the 19th century, had been brought into ever closer treaty relations with British India. British power in India was at its height, and a British peace reigned in Gulf waters.

This *Pax Britannica* was initially imposed by force in expeditions against the seafaring Qawasim of Ras al-Khaimah and Sharjah in 1809 and 1819-20. The British directed their two seaborne campaigns against the Qawasim because the latter were trying to end Britain's control of Gulf trade and were carrying on a maritime *jihad* in alliance with the Al Saud of

Najd. Such acts were perceived at the time as piracy, and threatened British communications and trade in the Gulf. In 1835 Britain persuaded the ruling shaikhs of the chief tribes inhabiting the southern shore of the Gulf, from Abu Dhabi to Ras al-Khaimah, to enter into a truce at sea during the pearling season. In return Britain undertook to police the truce and to maintain the maritime peace of the Gulf.

At first renewed annually, this truce was gradually elaborated and tightened up. The Ten-Year Truce of 1843-53 was a triumph of patient negotiation by the gifted Political Resident Samuel Hennell. In 1853 it was made permanent by the Perpetual Treaty of Maritime Peace, in which, in 1861, Bahrain was also included. In 1842 Britain had decided to put an end to the slave trade from East Africa, and began to enforce the ban in the Gulf by (largely ineffectual) naval patrols and treaties with the Shaikhs. Britain's principal motive, in maintaining the peace, was to secure her imperial communications via the Gulf route to India. This she aimed to do by minimal means, ensuring the peace at sea but avoiding, on the whole, being drawn into the local rulers' territorial disputes on land. For the local people of the "Trucial Coast" or "Trucial Oman", as the Emirates had by then come to be known, the peace brought the benefit of an improved pearl harvest and expanding pearl trade. This was some compensation as Britain, in also seeking to suppress the lucrative slave trade and, later, the arms trade, had in other ways adversely affected the economy of the coast.

The difficulties of early photography were satirised in this illustration in the Rev. Edward Bradley's *Photographic Pleasures Popularly Portrayed*, first published in London in 1855.

For much of the 19th century the internal politics of the Trucial Coast were dominated by the rivalry between, on the one hand, the Qasimi shaikhdom of Sharjah and Ras al-Khaimah, and the Bani Yas tribal confederacy of Abu Dhabi and Liwa on the other. The deep-seated Hinawi-Ghafiri tribal split, which had determined the politics of Oman since the 18th century, also ordained the allegiances of the coast tribes: the Bani Yas supported the Hinawi faction which included the Sultans of Muscat, while the Qawasim identified with the Ghafiri grouping. At times the Al Saud of Dir'iyyah and, after 1824, Riyadh, became involved in the shaikhdoms. When they and their followers – the austere Islamic reformers who followed the teachings of Shaikh

Muhammad bin 'Abd al-Wahhab – were trying to enlarge their role in south-east Arabia, they supported the Qawasim, as we have seen, and other tribes of the Ghafiri faction.

In the 1820s the most powerful ruler on the coast was Sultan bin Saqr, the greatest of the Qasimi chiefs, who ruled Sharjah and Ras al-Khaimah from 1803 till 1866, dying at the ripe old age of ninety-seven. Sharjah grew rapidly, and was the natural choice as location for the British Residency Agent when they decided to station one on the Coast, at first briefly from c.1823-25, and then from 1866 on. After Shaikh Sultan's death the Qasimi shaikhdom, which embraced the two coasts from Rams and Dibah in the north to Sharjah and Khor Kalba in the south, the hinterland between, and the port of Lingah on the Persian coast, declined, and the Bani Yas became predominant. By 1892 the rise of Persia had caused the

This view of Lingah, the formerly prosperous Qasimi port on the Persian coast, was taken c.1904-14 by an unknown photographer. The size and quality of the original photograph suggests a professional photographer, but it is also possible that it was taken by a British naval officer or official, many of whom had cameras by this time.

decline of Lingah, and disputes among the sons of Sultan bin Saqr had divided the Qasimi shaikhdom.

The Bani Yas originated in the Liwa Oasis as a tribal confederation. Having founded Abu Dhabi in the mid-18th century, they began to emerge after 1823 as a strong force on the Hinawi side, in opposition to the Ghafiri

Qawasim. In 1833 a split between the ruling Al Bu Falah (later Al Nahyan) and their kinsmen, the Al Bu Falasah, led to the latter leaving for Dubai, where the Al Maktum of Al Bu Falasah succeeded in making themselves masters. Thereafter Dubai pursued a course independent of Hinawi-Ghafiri rivalry, as far as possible steering clear of both the Bani Yas and Qawasim factions. In making commerce their priority, the Al Maktum in the 19th century were to emerge as the merchant princes of the Gulf.

Under Zayed bin Khalifah, who ruled from 1855 till 1909, Abu Dhabi grew as a political power, despite the relatively small size of its population, and controlled a large land area stretching from the base of the Qatar peninsula in the west to the area of Al-'Ain in the east. More land-based and pastoralist than the seafaring Qawasim, they nonetheless played a large role in the pearl fishery, which they came to dominate. By 1900 Zayed bin Khalifah's efforts to unify the shaikhdoms by alliance had made him the most politically influential ruler on the coast, while Dubai had risen to commercial supremacy, overtaking Sharjah.

The invention of photography in 1839 was just one facet of the accelerating technological revolution transforming 19th century Europe. Some of these advances had the effect of deepening Britain's involvement in the Gulf. As steam took over from sail, naval patrols became capable of a more rapid response. A steamship service was introduced by the British Indian Steam Navigation Company in 1862 which, while not calling on the Trucial Coast, provided an important new means of communication and cargo-carrying, although the bulk of the Gulf's trade continued to be carried by Arab craft. Although the Coast did not have a British Political Agent, a local Residency Agent was appointed at Sharjah in 1866 to look after the interests of the Indian traders, who were British subjects, on the Coast. The volume of trade was on the rise, and manufactured goods reaching the *suq*s of eastern Arabia increased, particularly textiles. In 1864 the first maritime telegraph cable was laid in the Gulf. It ran from Bombay to Jask on the Persian coast, and on to Bushire and Fao via the Musandam Peninsula, where there were cable stations at Ghubbat Ghazirah (Malcolm's Inlet) and Khor al-Sha'am (Elphinstone's Inlet). Such new developments meant that, while officials of the Government of India might seek to limit British intervention to the maintenance of the peace at sea, this arm's length policy was becoming increasingly difficult to maintain on the ground. This was particularly so because the new transport technologies were to make it easier for other nations to interfere in the Gulf.

By the 1860s the waters of the Gulf had been effectively closed by the British to the influence of outside powers. The Ottoman Turks, who for three hundred years had ruled Iraq, presented little threat and, in any case, Britain was anxious, for reasons to do with European politics, to maintain the *status quo* in the Ottoman lands. The only threat from that direction had come from Muhammad Ali of Egypt, himself once an Ottoman vassal but now dreaming of an Egyptian empire forged from Arabia and the Arab provinces of the Turkish Sultan. In 1837-9 he had invaded Najd and eastern Arabia, threatened Bahrain, and sent a Najdi representative to Sharjah as Egyptian governor of the Coast. But he was forced in 1840 to abandon his ambitions by an alliance of Britain, France, Prussia, Austria and Russia in support of the Ottoman Sultan. Persian aspirations on the northern Gulf coast had been dashed by defeat by the British in the Anglo-Persian War of 1856-7. The Persian threat was not in any case a maritime one; but the show of force by the British expeditionary force had a sobering effect on the Arabian shore.

So, in the 1860s, the tranquillity of the southern Gulf was disturbed only by local rivalries on land and by the renewal of Najdi ambitions in the area. Britain's political and commercial supremacy was assuming the appearance of a patiently planned and constructed edifice. This at any rate was how it appeared to outside powers, though it had in fact been built up over the decades less through the application of policy than by patient, cautious and empirical response to circumstances, particularly by the dogged Hennell and his successor as Resident, Kemball. By and large, Britain maintained its policy of not getting involved in disputes on land, though difficulties in Bahrain and Oman were beginning to make the line between peace at sea and peace on land an impossible one to discern.

Then, in 1871, the first tremor shook the structure: the Ottoman invasion and occupation of al-Hasa. By the late 1880s there were more alarming ripples on the calm surface of this exclusive "British lake", as foreign powers saw it. A resurgent Persia was seeking to develop its navy, and hence its power to interfere, in the Gulf. This led the British, in 1887, to extract an assurance from the shaikhs of the Trucial Coast that they would not enter into an agreement with any power other than Britain.

For British interests this was a timely move. By 1891, the presence of two French agents, one named Chapuy, on the Trucial Coast impelled the British to conclude an Exclusive Treaty with the shaikhs, which was signed in 1892. During the course of the 1890s France's negotiations to obtain a coaling depot near Muscat, and her relationship with the sailors of Sur in the Sharqiyyah, were leading, much to British dismay, to a deepening French involvement in Oman. By concluding the Exclusive Agreement, Britain left the shaikhdoms domestically autonomous but effectively barred the shaikhs from conducting their own foreign affairs; in return, Britain took responsibility for their defence and external relations. The scene was set for the deepening involvement on land which was to characterise Britain's relations with the shaikhdoms during the 20th century. For the Exclusive Treaty was to form the basis of Britain's relationship with the Trucial States right up till her withdrawal from the Gulf in 1971.

In the late 1890s, Russia and Germany too sought to establish a presence in the Gulf. Both began to explore, in collaboration with the Ottomans, the possibility of reaching the Gulf by means of a rail-link via Baghdad to Basra and Kuwait. Between 1899 and 1903, Russia sent a series of naval vessels annually to Muscat, Bandar Abbas, Bushire, Bahrain, Kuwait and Basra to impress the rulers and create goodwill in preparation for extending her influence in more tangible ways. In 1901 Russia set up new consulates at Basra and Bushire. In the ports of the Gulf, notably Kuwait, Bahrain and Lingah, European agents began to set up in business. In Bahrain and Lingah, for example, the Hamburg import-export firm of Wönckhaus and Co. established offices, and set about acquiring concessions for red-oxide mining on Abu Musa Island and Hormuz.

Cameras, which although still expensive had continued to be modified and improved throughout the 1890s, were by 1900 far from rare in the Gulf, being brought there by the British, French, Russians and Germans involved in the various schemes. In 1893, the German archaeologist, ethnographer and government agent Dr Max Freiherr von Oppenheim visited and collected photographs of Bushire, Lingah, Bandar Abbas and Muscat. Russian naval personnel took pictures at their ports of call and, in 1902, a Russian zoologist named Nicholas Bogoyavlensky, who spent much of 1902 in Kuwait, Bahrain and Muscat, was reported by a British Agent as having taken photographs in Kuwait. In 1903 André Jouannin, the Secretary-General of the Comité de l'Asie Française, took many photographs on his exploratory tour of the Gulf, which took him to Muscat, the Persian coast, Bahrain, Bushire, Hormuz, back to Muscat and thence to Aden.

As ever, those with mankind's spiritual wellbeing at heart came hard on the heels of those with more worldly concerns. In the case of the Gulf, the initiative was taken by the Arabian Mission of the Dutch Reformed Church in America. The Arabian Mission had been founded in 1889 in New Brunswick by James Cantine and Samuel Zwemer. In 1892-3 they established three medical mission stations, at Basra, Bahrain and Muscat, from which they made extensive tours around the region. Missionaries were often keen amateur photographers, and Samuel Zwemer was no exception. In 1900 and 1901 he made three journeys through the shaikhdoms and northern Oman: the first took him overland from Sharjah to Shinas and Suhar on the Batinah coast of Oman; the second by sea from Abu Dhabi to Sharjah; and the third overland from Abu Dhabi to Suhar by way of the region of Al-'Ain. The only way to reach the Coast, he

Open.   Closed.

Folding cameras of the type popular by the turn of the century. Different models were available for glass plates, stiff films or roll film.

remarked, was by dhow, in his case from Bahrain via Dalma Island, the importance of which not just for pearling but also as a market for pearl traders he confirms. He was received with great hospitality wherever he went, especially by Shaikh Zayed at Abu Dhabi where, as we have seen, he photographed the fort. He noted that Sharjah, though still a Wahhabi centre, was without fanaticism, and that the growing town of Dubai was the "real metropolis of northern Oman. … At the present rate of growth, Dubai will outstrip all the other towns, and soon be a port of call for steamers".

Many of Dr Zwemer's photographs of his extensive journeys in the Arab lands are known to exist in the Archives of the Reformed Church in America, as are later photographs by his colleagues. However, they await proper identification and cataloguing before it can be determined whether any of the pictures taken on his early journeys in the shaikhdoms have survived.

In 1902, Percy Cox arrived on the scene. Cox was Britain's Political Agent at Muscat from 1899 to 1904 – the start of a career which was to make him a celebrity amongst the Gulf Arabs (who knew him as "Cokus"),

Percy Cox at Basra in 1916. By this time Cox had been British Resident in the Persian Gulf for almost a decade (1904-13), and was now Chief Political Officer of the Mesopotamian Expeditionary Force. (Gertrude Bell)

and which was to culminate in the early 1920s with his appointment as High Commissioner in Iraq. Cox had started to take photographs in Somaliland in the late 1890s, where he used a variety of Club cameras from the London firm of Adams and Co. In 1902 he took photographs on a journey from Abu Dhabi via Al-'Ain and Jabal Akhdar to Muscat, although only a single one from the Trucial Coast appears to have survived. He arrived at his starting-point by sea from Muscat, in *HMS Redbreast*, a small gunboat, and was accompanied on this part of the journey by the Sultan in his steam yacht *Nur al-Bahr*, as the Sultan had business with Shaikh Zayed bin Khalifah, "the grand old man of the Pirate Coast", as Cox calls him. They passed along the fringe of the great pearl banks, where Cox notes Britain's role in protecting the fishery from outside interference and internal disruption. They were then well received at Abu Dhabi by Shaikh Zayed, who put on a special display of horsemanship on the sands behind the town. Cox's single surviving photograph of Abu Dhabi in 1902 shows the Shaikh and his sons dismounting after this event.

After obtaining the Shaikh's permission to travel on to Al-'Ain, he was shown round the town. His visit was brief for:

About 2pm my camels began to arrive, but it was 5pm before we got away. Shaikh Zaid accompanied me for a short distance and sent his son Sagar [*Saqr*] with me as far as Maqta, the ford across the tidal creek 10 miles from the town. Sagar was a handsome and intelligent young man, thirsting for knowledge of the great world, and … the chief topics of our conversation were the development of wireless and the idea, recently mooted by the late Rev. J.H. Bacon, the aeronaut, of crossing the Great Arabian Desert by balloon … Sagar left me about 8.30pm on his own side of the creek, and I just managed to get across with the water up to my girths, guided by the old caretaker of the tower which stands in mid-stream to guard the ford.

If there was a reaction to the notion of a Reverend Bacon flying over the Rub' al-Khali in a balloon, Cox does not record it. Cox reached Buraimi after forty hours travelling and, after a short stay, pressed on to the Shaikh of Abu Dhabi's settlements at Jahili and Al-'Ain, whence he followed a route parallel to Jabal Hafit. From there he travelled through Ibri and the Jabal Akhdar of Oman. He then had to hurry on to Muscat to join the cruiser *Amphitrite* for an official tour of the Gulf – as an antidote to the Russian visits, in particular that of the cruiser *Varyag* a few months previously.

In 1904 Cox was appointed British Consul and Resident at Bushire, and so became Britain's most important official in the Gulf. From there, in 1905, he undertook a second journey into the interior of south-east Arabia, the purpose of which was to establish the latitude and longitude of the area of Al-'Ain for Fraser Hunter's map being produced by the Survey of India. This time he took Ras al-Khaimah as his starting-point, landing there with his assistant and his instruments, camera included. They easily obtained camels in the town, and were accommodated in the Shaikh's fort, where a large crowd assembled to see them leave for the interior the next day. Once again, only one photograph survives from the part of this journey in the shaikhdoms, and it is of this crowd outside the fort.

They followed the ordinary caravan route via the Sir district, Ras al-Khaimah's agricultural hinterland, where Cox notes that there were ten villages containing some 2500 inhabitants and about 10,000 date trees. After that they went via the oasis of Dhaid, then as now in Sharjah territory, watered by its fine *falaj*. The people of Dhaid were drawn from the Bani Qitab, Na'im and Tanaij. Thereafter they followed the inland plain of the Dhahirah south to Al-'Ain, which they entered from the north-west "through the recently formed Bani Yas colony of Mas'udi", and camped at Jimi. Most trade from Al-'Ain, it

seems, was no longer with Suhar on the Batinah of Oman, but with Sharjah and Dubai. As Zwemer had predicted, Dubai was now a port of call for British India Company steamers. At Buraimi the Na'im still occupied their special position as of old, but Cox observes that Abu Dhabi's possessions and influence were increasing year by year. Having fixed Buraimi's position, Cox and his assistant left Buraimi to rejoin his ship at Suhar.

In the interval between Cox's two journeys, the Trucial Coast was visited by the German traveller Hermann Burchardt. Burchardt came of a wealthy Jewish family in Berlin, and his private means enabled him to travel extensively in all five continents. In 1890 his growing interest in the Islamic East led him to the study of Arabic. He eventually settled in Damascus, which he used as base for his extensive travels throughout Syria, Mesopotamia, Persia, Arabia and East Africa. In Arabia, as well as his journey down the Gulf which concerns us here, he made several journeys in the Yemen until his murder there in 1909. An accomplished scholar, Burchardt was also a capable photographer, who worked mainly on glass.

In the winter of 1903-4 Burchardt set off down the coast of eastern

Shaikh Zayed bin Khalifah and his sons, Abu Dhabi 1902. A note on the back of this photograph in Cox's handwriting reads: "Pirate Coast: the Shaikh of Abu Thabi and his stalwart sons. The Shaikh has just dismounted, sons on horseback." Cox noted that Shaikh Zayed was over eighty years old, while Zwemer, the year before, said he was well preserved, with "twelve sons and the full number of wives". Cox is known to have owned Adams and Company Club Cameras since the late 1890s, with rapid rectilinear and wide-angle lenses, although this picture is not one of his best efforts. (Cox 1902)

the interior flocked to visit him, all curious to investigate this German traveller and his belongings – most especially his camera and photographs. "As already mentioned, I was forbidden to take photographs," he tells us, "but while showing and explaining the apparatus, I managed to fix on the plate one of the Arabs who had come from Buraimi."

On 17th February the Shaikh returned and made it clear that Burchardt's presence in the town was unwelcome. Five days later Burchardt boarded a *battil* bound for the Batinah coast and Muscat, and bade the Trucial Coast farewell.

Burchardt's visit to eastern Arabia in 1903-4 took place in the wake of the voyage of Lord Curzon, the Viceroy of India, round the ports of the Gulf. The flurry of Russian, German and French activity had alarmed Curzon, who championed a more assertive policy in defence of British interests. The chief ports were already regularly visited by British political and naval officers but, by 1903, Curzon had decided that the time had come for a more ostentatious assertion of British hegemony. Accordingly, he set out on a grand progress round the Gulf to impress the people of the littoral and their Shaikhs with the unassailable power of the Great Government, since some of them had shown themselves worryingly susceptible to foreign overtures. He made his viceregal tour aboard *RIMS*

The German traveller Hermann Burchardt (left) is shown here in San'a, Yemen, probably in 1907-9. His luggage, which was heavy and bulky, probably contained a good deal of photographic equipment, including a camera stand and a quality folding camera taking half-plate glass negatives. (Burchardt)

Burchardt insisted on making his Gulf journey aboard local craft rather than the steamer service, and left Dubai on this boat, which he calls a *battil* (it is in fact the very similar but more common type, the *baqqarah*). (Burchardt 1904)

Arabia, shunning the regular steamer service in favour of small, local craft. After visiting Kuwait and Bahrain, he took ship for 'Uqayr on the Hasa coast and went inland to Hasa Oasis. From Hofuf he travelled overland to Doha in Qatar, and took a boat to Abu Dhabi, which he reached on 2nd February 1904. On landing he was taken straight away to see Shaikh Zayed, who was holding his *majlis*. On completion of the day's business, the Shaikh offered Burchardt food and accommodation, and this hospitality was extended to Burchardt throughout his six-day stay in the town. He was allowed to walk about and take photographs, noting that "only on the first day was I troubled by shrieks and mockery … but a command of the Shaikh sufficed to control this nuisance."

Burchardt then sailed on to Dubai, where his reception by the ruling family was very different. One can only speculate on the reasons for this, as he seems to have been given no explanation. On his arrival he was received by Shaikh Maktum's young son, who was deputising for his father during a brief absence. Burchardt was left to wander round the town alone, but was forbidden to take photographs. He noted a certain wealth about the place, attributing this – correctly – to the Shaikh's astute decision to declare Dubai a duty-free port. In the evenings people from the town and

Burchardt was well received in Abu Dhabi by the Shaikh, whom he photographed holding his open-air *majlis* outside the fort. By this time Shaikh Zayed had ruled for almost fifty years, and had five more years ahead of him. (Burchardt 1904)
Right **Burchardt was able to take only one stealthy photograph in Dubai, of this Arab tribesman who came to investigate the strange foreign traveller and his curious photographic apparatus. (Burchardt 1904)**

Argonaut, a large warship which, with its four funnels and six accompanying ships, was deemed a sufficiently potent statement to erase the impression made late the previous year by the five-funnelled Russian warship *Askold*. After visiting Muscat, Curzon held a durbar off Sharjah on 21st November 1903 which was attended by the Shaikhs of Abu-

Dhabi, Sharjah, Dubai, 'Ajman and Umm al-Qaiwain. His voyage took in the Arabian shore up to Kuwait, the return being made via Bushire on the Persian side. Both official and unofficial photographs were taken throughout the tour, some of them being preserved amongst Lord Curzon's photographic collections at the India Office Library in London.

Throughout his life Lord Curzon maintained a great enthusiasm for photography. In the early 1890s he began to use one of the new Kodak cameras which had been developed by George Eastman and which, by the turn of the century, had greatly reduced the cost and complications of photography. These simple snapshot cameras with their celluloid roll film – which after 1891 could be loaded and unloaded in daylight – were an enormous success and brought hundreds and thousands of newcomers to photography, including some of the British naval officers whose task it was to police the waters of the Gulf.

Russian schemes in the Gulf were curtailed in 1903 by the growing tension in the Far East which led to the Russo-Japanese War. At the same time hostile French designs were nullified in 1904 by the Entente Cordiale between Britain and France. However, German and Ottoman threats to the exclusive British sphere of influence disappeared only in 1918 with the end of the First World War. The years up to 1914 and the outbreak of war between Britain and Germany were marked by Britain's deepening involvement in the internal affairs of the Gulf. However autonomous the Shaikhs might be on land, Britain was inevitably drawn into territorial disputes amongst them, and there was increasing concern about the affairs of the interior following Cox's visits of 1902 and 1905. Britain continued to develop her communications: during Cox's time as Resident he tried to have a wireless station erected at Dubai, though this was rejected by the Shaikh. Cox also wished to appoint a British officer at Sharjah instead of the local Residency Agent 'Abd al-Latif bin 'Abd al-Rahman, though once

Lord Curzon's durbar off Sharjah on 21st November 1903, aboard *RIMS Argonaut*. Curzon sits on the raised dais, with assembled shaikhs from Abu Dhabi, Sharjah, Dubai, 'Ajman and Umm al-Qaiwain facing him. The picture is from a series collected by Curzon as a record of his viceregal tour of the Gulf. By this time the Royal Navy had many trained photographers among its officers, one of whom probably took this picture. (Curzon Collection, 1903)

again he failed in this owing to the ruling family's resistance. The policy of keeping out German and Turkish influence continued, as evidenced by Cox's role in the Shaikh of Sharjah's cancellation of Wönckhaus's red oxide concession in 1906.

Britain was also still actively involved in the suppression of the slave and arms trades. The result was growing tension in relations with the Shaikhs, the climax of which came with the Dubai Incident in December 1910, when the people of Dubai and a squad of British marines clashed in the town during a search for arms. The trade in arms had shifted to Dubai because of British success in suppressing it on the Omani coast. By this time Dubai had grown into a major commercial centre, partly as a result of its duty-free status, but also because of a recent influx of Arab merchants fleeing from the oppression of Persian rule in Lingah, and the long-term silting up of Sharjah's creek. The pearl trade was flourishing, and the new wealth began to bring more contact with the outside world. Indian traders who were British subjects settled in growing numbers in the ports, especially Dubai which, since 1902, had become a port of call for steamships.

Despite the gradual ending of its long isolation, the Trucial Coast still seems to have been seldom visited by photographers, however. Apart from Gouldsmith's, few naval officers' photographs of the shaikhdoms are at present known from this period. The Coast was not actively involved in the British campaign to eject the Turks from Mesopotamia which played such an important part in the 1914-18 War, and which has bequeathed to us an enormous body of historic photography of Iraq. Of the many British troopships which plied the Gulf between India and Basra during the War, few if any seem to have stopped on the Trucial Coast. A cargo steamer – the Persian Gulf Navigation Company's *SS Zaiyanni* – is on record as having called at Dubai in 1916, but such records are rare, and few photographs have come to light. Likewise, few pictures taken by Royal Navy personnel on patrol in the Gulf seem to have survived from this time.

With the defeat of Germany and the collapse of the Russian and Ottoman Empires, Britain during the 1920s reached the zenith of her power in the Middle East. The grant of League of Nations mandates for Palestine and Iraq gave international recognition of her power, which was further shown by her ability to establish the Emirate of Transjordan in 1921, and to instal a monarchy in Iraq in the same year.

In the Gulf she was unchallenged by her pre-War rivals. Moreover, the prospects of oil discovery gave Britain for the first time a direct economic interest there. Determining the frontiers of the newly emergent states of Iraq, Kuwait and Najd (or, as it was to become after 1932, Saudi Arabia), had become an urgent priority, not least in order to clarify sovereignty over concession areas to be leased to the oil companies who were now

A collection of portable hand cameras, including a folding Pocket Kodak, the simplicity and low cost of which brought photography to many thousands of people during the first two decades of the 20th century.

interested in eastern Arabia. The early negotiations over the Iraq, Najd and Kuwait frontiers were pushed through, in his customary magisterial style, by Sir Percy Cox. Further south, in the Trucial States, the question of land frontiers with Najd and Oman was left till the 1930s. The consequence was to be decades of wrangling, fuelled by oil company rivalry: by 1971 a solution satisfactory to all parties was still eluding them.

The Anglo-Persian Oil Company (APOC, later British Petroleum), which had begun producing oil in commercial quantities before the War at Masjid-i-Sulayman, resumed its exploration activities in the 1920s. Arnold Wilson, who had served under Cox in Mesopotamia, and later as Civil Commissioner in Iraq, visited the Trucial Coast as a representative of APOC, and took photographs there in 1926.

By the late 1920s cameras were becoming as commonplace as typewriters in both Europe and America. Ever more complex and expensive models were being used by those professionals and scholars whose work involved the collection of visual data, for example the British Royal Air Force, the embryonic civil aviation companies, the oil companies, and

Right This early picture of the waterfront at Sharjah was taken c.1907-9 by the British naval officer Lieut.-Commander A.N. Gouldsmith, using a snapshot camera. Snapshot cameras encouraged people with no previous experience to take up photography and to take pictures in circumstances which would have deterred a professional. Snapshots, though often poor in quality, could provide a more detailed and truthful picture than the polished work of a professional aiming to produce an aesthetically pleasing image. By 1903 a wide range of snapshot cameras was available.

A boarding party prepares to search a typical gun-running dhow in the southern Gulf. Her sails are riddled with holes made by the shells fired to stop her. This picture was taken by an unknown British naval man involved in the blockade of the Gulf which took place between 1912 and 1914

archaeologists and anthropologists. Both the RAF and the oil companies undertook wide-ranging aerial photographic surveys in the Middle East during the 1920s and 1930s. At the same time snapshot cameras had become cheaper, and between 1914 and 1920 sales increased fivefold, a trend which continued, surprisingly, through the Depression years of the 1930s.

Photography's range was of course continuously being extended as it was put to new uses, and during the 1920s it entered a new phase as it began to concern itself with social issues, as well as scientific visual recording. The reputation of photography increased as advances were made in camera design – in 1924, for example, Oscar Barnack completed work on the Leica lightweight camera, which incorporated the means to control exposure, took thirty-six pictures, and had an astigmatic lens. This small, compact yet exceedingly sophisticated camera offered both amateurs and professionals a combination of spontaneity and quality which had never been achievable in photography before. Thanks to such cameras photojournalism and the illustrated magazine later began to enjoy their heyday.

The use of photography for systematic data recording in Arabia can be seen in the work of Bertram Thomas. Thomas, a young British political officer, was appointed in 1925 as Financial Adviser and Wazir to Sayyid Taimur ibn Faisal, the Sultan of Muscat and Oman – an appointment which was symptomatic of Britain's deepening involvement in the internal affairs of south-east Arabia. Thomas had served with Arnold Wilson and Gertrude Bell in Iraq at the end of the War. His appointment to Oman placed him in a uniquely strong position for a foreigner: he could go where he liked and pursue his varied interests with the protection of the Sultan. Since he spoke Arabic well and was an accomplished photographer, whose interests lay in exploration, anthropology and linguistics, his posting represented a rich opportunity. In the winter of 1930-31, after various journeys which included a trip from Suhar to Sharjah in 1927, he achieved fame by becoming the first non-Arab to cross the Rub' al-Khali.

Unfortunately, though much of Thomas's archive has survived in the Royal Geographical Society, in the Royal Anthropological Institute in London and in the Middle East Centre at Cambridge University, most of the pictures he took on the Suhar-Sharjah journey, if indeed he took many, have either disappeared or are now unidentifiable, other than those which appear in *Alarms and Excursions in Arabia*. This journey, the purpose of which was to reconnoitre for landing places for the Basra-Karachi air route, took him past Buraimi, which he had to avoid due to the presence there of a mission from Riyadh laying claim to the oasis. Instead he went to Mahdah, the seat of the Bani Ka'ab, who once owed a fluctuating allegiance to Umm al-Qaiwain, and thence through the territory of the Bani Qitab, a Sharjah tribe, passing Jabal Fayyah. It was a hard journey in the heat of the summer, and Thomas comments on the poverty of the land. Near Sharjah he was joined by a shaikh of the Awamir, who told him that "he would not change his hungry and thirsty existence plus his liberty for all the fleshpots of a settled life and its bondage". He reached Sharjah in early June, but there was trouble in the town and he did not linger, making instead for a British ship lying offshore. As he puts it: "in ten minutes I had felt, learned, and tasted the luxury of electric fans, the latest Test Match news, and the amenities of the ward-room."

Another visitor in the late 1920s was the British seaman Herbert Vaughan. Vaughan served in the Royal Navy from 1911 to 1945, and did a tour of the Gulf in 1928-30 as Paymaster Lieutenant-Commander on *HMS Triad*, on which he was secretary to the Senior Naval Officer, Persian Gulf Station. His interest was the traditional sailing craft of the Gulf and Oman, and he was perhaps the first photographer to attempt a full coverage of all the different types of vessel.

During the 1920s the people of Abu Dhabi, Dubai and Sharjah were emerging from their previous isolation, and were better educated and informed about world events. In touch with developments in Bombay and Cairo, many were eager for progress and some were suspicious of what they took to be Britain's imperial motives. However, the worldwide depression of 1929 was a bitter blow to the economy of the Coast. Schools

"Loyal chiefs" come alongside the Royal navy ship *HMS Fox* at Khor Fakkan, 1917-18 – one of the few photographs of the shaikhdoms during the First World War. The title and quality of this picture suggest it was taken by a trained photographer sent to make a record of naval activities in the Gulf. (IWM HU. 67687)

were closed and many rich pearl merchants became bankrupt. The pearl trade never recovered because, in the 1930s, the Japanese development of the cultured pearl destroyed whatever market there might have been for Gulf pearls.

The 1930s were therefore a time of hardship, and people began to emigrate in search of work. The only ray of hope was the prospect of oil discovery: big strikes in Bahrain, Kuwait and Saudi Arabia throughout the 1930s suggested that the Trucial Coast might be the next to benefit. Britain had remained unchallenged in the Gulf only until 1928, when the success of United States oil companies in gaining concessions first in Bahrain and then in al-Hasa, as a result of the "open-door" policy, began to undermine her pre-eminence. The British were anxious to protect their interests in the shaikhdoms, and the first oil concession there was finally granted, in the face of US rivalry, to Petroleum Development (Trucial Coast), an associate of the Iraq Petroleum Company, by Dubai in 1937. Although US interests held nearly a quarter share in IPC, as did Dutch and French interests, the management of IPC lay in British hands. By 1939 Sharjah, Ras al-Khaimah, Abu Dhabi and 'Ajman had also granted concessions, and seasonal geological surveys were begun.

The search for oil and its discovery in al-Hasa in 1938, and the rapid expansion of ARAMCO after the Second World War, lent a new importance to the traditional dispute over the allegiance of the Buraimi

tribes: the question of control over territory in the Rub' al-Khali, where oil discoveries might be made, injected a new heat into the dispute between Abu Dhabi and Saudi Arabia. As Abu Dhabi's protector, Britain was inevitably drawn into the dispute on the side of her *protegé*; at the same time she felt that concessions had to be made to Ibn Saud. The negotiations remained unresolved in the 1930s as the Second World War put a temporary stop to the debate.

While Saudi Arabia was emerging as the dominant power in the Peninsula, on the other side of the Gulf, in the 1920s, Persian aspirations were also having to be considered by Britain. In the 1920s Persia established a navy on the Gulf, revoked after 1931 her agreement to grant landing grounds for aircraft, and pressed the British to move their Political Residency from Bushire and their naval base from Henjam. On behalf of the Qasimi shaikhdoms of Sharjah and Ras al-Khaimah, Britain had to resist Persian claims to the Gulf islands of Abu Musa and the Tanbs.

Another factor which deepened British involvement was the development of the Gulf air route to India, which in the early days was to go by a variety of different routes between Basra and Karachi. The search for a viable route and suitable landing grounds generated the first aerial

Left Lt.-Col. Sir Arnold T. Wilson in c.1920, when he was Civil Commissioner in Mesopotamia. Bertram Thomas served under Wilson in Iraq at the end of the First World War. Wilson recorded his travels on a snapshot camera. (From Bertram Thomas, *Alarms and Excursions in Arabia*)
Right Bertram Thomas on his favourite camel "Khuwarah" at around the time of his journey from Suhar to Sharjah in 1927. Thomas was a capable photographer who used a quality camera taking 4¼ x 6½ inch negatives – possibly a Folding Kodak. But by his time mass production techniques and the use of new materials to replace wood – notably bakelite and aluminium – were bringing cameras to an ever-growing mass market. (Bertram Thomas)

Thomas had to avoid Buraimi in 1927 and instead went via Mahdah, the outskirts of which are shown here, on his journey to Sharjah. Today in Oman, Mahdah was the seat of the Bani Ka'ab, who, with the Bani Qitab of Dhaid and the Na'im of Buraimi, were one of the principal tribes of the Dhahirah. They had owed allegiance to Umm al-Qaiwain in the early part of the 20th century, but now acknowledged the Sultan of Muscat and Oman.

A *baqqarah* drawn up amongst the waterfront *barasti* houses at Sharjah in July 1929 by H.R. Vaughan. Vaughan's survey of Arabian Gulf craft illustrates two longstanding trends among British naval officers with photographic training: the propensity to make portraits of vessels, which began as far back as the 1840s, and the use of photography for systematic survey work of all types.

photography of the Trucial States. As we have seen, in 1927 Britain had tried initially to establish the route via the Arabian side of the Gulf, with stops at Abu Dhabi, Mahdah and Suhar. This was deemed too risky because of trouble in the hinterland. In 1929 a route was agreed along the Persian coast of the Gulf, but this in turn had to be abandoned at Persian insistence after 1931. From 1932 a new Arabian route came into being, after negotiations with the Shaikhs, and Sharjah was chosen as the airfield on the Trucial Coast. This gave a temporary boost to Sharjah's economy.

By the end of the 1930s Dubai, which had suffered badly during the commercial depression of the 1930s, and Abu Dhabi also had re-fuelling facilities for flying boats.

In photography the trends established during the 1920s continued in the 1930s. There was a further huge increase in the sale of snapshot cameras and film while, at the professional level, many newspapers were now illustrating their reports with photographs. This was the decade that saw the launch of *Life* magazine in America and *Picture Post* in Britain.

An early aerial shot of Dubai, taken in January 1931 on a survey flight for the Gulf air route. A suitable landing area for flying boats is marked on the Creek.

Wilfred Thesiger in 1948, during his second crossing of the Rub' al-Khali. (Thesiger) In 1950 Thesiger again went hunting with Shaikh Zayed bin Sultan around Al-'Ain. Here Thesiger dramatically captures the falcon shielding its prey - a *houbara* bustard. Like all other wildlife, the *houbara* is today a rarity owing to over-hunting. (Thesiger)

Technical innovations included automatic exposure control, which was the subject of many patents, and the flashbulb. Both of these developments were to influence the design of cameras for the popular market after the Second World War.

By the time the Second World War broke out in 1939, Britain's interests, now not only strategic but also economic, meant that she was involved in the shaikhdoms as never before. However, the War brought a lull in oil exploration and continued the standstill in trade. This brought many people, particularly in Dubai, to the brink of starvation, alleviated only by the supply of food contributed by Britain. Whereas in the First World War the Gulf witnessed the Mesopotamia campaign, in the 1939-45 War it was not close to any arena of conflict. For the local people the War represented a hiatus in development, and stagnation brought a continuation of pre-War hardships. Immediately after the War hostilities broke out between Abu Dhabi and Dubai and continued till 1948, making it dangerous to travel in the hinterland. Hard times exacerbated the lawlessness of the tribesmen, and raiding was on the increase.

Meanwhile, in the aftermath of the War, Britain's imperial commitments were beginning to undergo the process of fundamental readjustment which, in the Gulf, was to end with her complete withdrawal in 1971. In withdrawing from India in 1947, she ended an era in imperial communications for which the Gulf had been so essential. Henceforth Gulf affairs were placed under direct administration from London rather than, as they had been before, under the British Government of India.

Paradoxically, this larger process of withdrawal from the East was fundamentally at odds with the local trend on the Trucial Coast. There Britain's involvement in fact continued to deepen throughout the same period: British economic interests in the shaikhdoms were set to expand greatly in the two decades after 1945. Reflecting this, in 1949 a permanent British Political Officer was appointed at Sharjah for the first time, replacing the local Residency Agent. In 1953 this post was raised to the status of Political Agent, and in 1954 the Agency was moved to Dubai, which was quickly regaining its old prosperity and eclipsing Sharjah once again. In 1957 a Political Officer was appointed in Abu Dhabi, and this post in turn was raised to the status of Political Agency in 1961.

Apart from anything else, it had become pressing to ensure the safety of oil company operations and personnel and of the airfields. In 1951, with the cooperation of the Rulers, a force called the Trucial Oman Levies was raised for the general maintenance of law and order and the protection of the shaikhdoms from external aggression. Led by British seconded officers, financed by Britain and headquartered at Sharjah, the TOL's strength soon grew to 1000 men, and they came to be known as the Trucial Oman Scouts. Among other things, the Scouts played a vital role in upholding Abu Dhabi's sovereignty. As a result the level of internal security was higher which meant that onshore exploration could begin again. Petroleum Development (Trucial States) held the onshore and offshore concessions for almost all the shaikhdoms. The first well was spudded in 1950 and the search went on throughout the 1950s, until the first oil in commercial quantities was struck in 1960 at Murban in Abu Dhabi territory.

The chief exceptions to PD(TC)'s concession coverage were the offshore areas of Abu Dhabi and Dubai. In 1948 Shaikh Shakhbut of Abu Dhabi had awarded the offshore concession to Superior Oil Company of California. In 1953 Superior relinquished it to Abu Dhabi Marine Areas Limited (ADMA), a new company owned two-thirds by BP and one-third by French interests, which also formed Dubai Marine Areas to operate the Dubai offshore concession.

Oil and security, both external and internal, brought an unprecedented influx of Britons to the Trucial States. This post-War period – from 1945 till the early 1960s – marks both the climax and the end of the early photography of the area. Until that time traditional life outside the major towns had changed very little. Not only that, photographic techniques and equipment reached a recognisably modern level, and colour photography became commonplace. After 1960 the first oil revenues began the accelerating transformation of the seven shaikhdoms into the modern state of the United Arab Emirates, as they were to become on British withdrawal from the Gulf in 1971.

The photography of this period encompasses the whole range, from the diplomat's snapshots of Sir Rupert Hay, the Political Resident in the Gulf (1941 and 1946-53) who was famous among his colleagues for his Box Brownie camera, to the highly professional work of oil company photographers. But the most important work of the immediate post-War period was by two gifted amateurs, the explorer Wilfred Thesiger, and the oil company man Ronald Codrai. Photographically, these are the years of Thesiger and Codrai, and it is to them that we now turn.

Thesiger first arrived in the Trucial States in 1946, at the end of the first of his two crossings of the Empty Quarter. By then he was already an experienced explorer. He had made his first important journey in the Danakil region of Abyssinia in 1933. In 1935 he joined the Sudan Political Service and, in 1940, the Sudan Defence Force, taking part in the Abyssinia campaign. From there he went to Jabal Druze in Syria, and went on campaign with the SAS in the Western Desert, returning to Abyssinia in 1945. In Addis Ababa he met O.B. Lean, the desert locust specialist of the Food and Agriculture Organisation in Rome. Lean was looking for someone to travel to the Rub' al-Khali to collect information on locust movements. Thesiger willingly accepted the challenge and, late the following year, after some preliminary travels in Najd, Asir and the Qara mountains of Dhufar, he made his first crossing of the great desert from Mughshin to the southern edge of the Liwa Oasis in Abu Dhabi territory. Here he turned eastwards into Oman, through what was to be the disputed frontier area, near Umm al-Zamul.

After his return in early 1947, he began to plan a second crossing of the Empty Quarter which would take him, in early 1948, via Wadi Dawasir and Jabrin in Saudi Arabia, to Liwa again. As the first European to visit Liwa, he would have liked to explore it at leisure, but the party's camels were exhausted and they continued to Abu Dhabi. His reception there by Shaikh Shakhbut and his brothers Hazza and Khalid was courteous and friendly, and his party enjoyed the Shaikh's hospitality for twenty days, during which he was at liberty to photograph the town. On 2nd April 1948 he left Abu Dhabi and four days later arrived at Muwaiqih where he stayed for almost a month as guest of Shaikh Zayed bin Sultan, today the President of the United Arab Emirates. He completed his journey with visits to Sharjah and Dubai, where he took several photographs before leaving by sea for Bahrain.

Thesiger returned to Muwaiqih in November 1948, and spent a month travelling through Liwa and the Dhafrah. He also enjoyed a month's hunting with Shaikh Zayed, who assisted him with his three-month, 1100-mile journey in Oman in early 1949. His next plan was to explore the Jabal Akhdar of Oman and, in pursuit of this, he returned to Muwaiqih in November 1949. His plans were thwarted, however, and he completed his visit on the coast, basing himself in Dubai, where he stayed with Edward Henderson, the representative of Petroleum Concessions (Trucial Coast), and his young assistant Ronald Codrai.

Thesiger had first acquired a Leica II camera in 1934, since its strong, compact design made it ideal for his long and arduous journeys where supplies had to be kept to a minimum. This was the camera he used until 1959, including his Arabian travels, where he found that the ideal way to protect it from sand was to keep it in a goatskin bag, as the bedouin did with their rifles. He later wrote that, at first, he had not taken his photography seriously, and that it was only on his first visit to southern Arabia in 1945 that he began to appreciate the value of the medium. He worked at first with a standard lens and yellow filter, adding an Elmarit/90 portrait lens and an Elmarit/35 wide-angle lens in the 1950s. By the late 1950s photography had become the chief means by which he recorded his

journeys, and he found his extensive collection of earlier photographs an essential tool in his later writings. With Thesiger's journeys between 1945 and 1950, therefore, one might say that photography at last attained equality with writing as a record of Arabian travel.

Although Thesiger always expressed a preference for portraiture, the most telling pictures for the historian are those which capture the old way of life, now gone. Thesiger's Arabian photographs show him not only to be a master at this, but an artist too. He brings a strong, instinctive sense of composition to his scenes of everyday life, of customs and regular activities, and so builds up a striking picture of many of the timeless and abiding features of old Arabia, its people and their relationship with their demanding land: weekly markets in their setting, bedouin at camp and on the move, drawing water from desert and oasis wells, livestock, cultivation techniques, villages, towns and ports, wildlife which is now almost extinct, and life on board a dhow, to take a few examples. With a few exceptions, the photographs presented here are previously unpublished.

It is easy to detect Thesiger's sophisticated eye for a photograph as an artistic composition in the way he talks about black-and-white photography, to which he has maintained a lifelong loyalty. "I have never taken a colour photograph," he wrote in 1987, "nor have I ever felt the urge to do so. This may be due in part to my preference for drawings rather than paintings, my appreciation of line rather than colour. … With black-and-white film … each subject offers its own variety of possibilities, according to the use made by the photographer of light and shade."

So much has been published about Ronald Codrai and his photographs that it would be superfluous to write at length about him here. He first arrived on the Trucial Coast travelling on his own, and then joined the oil company Petroleum Concessions (Trucial Coast) in 1948, working at first as deputy to Edward Henderson, before taking over from him in 1951. He lived in Dubai until 1955. A keen photographer from the start, his pictures record a crucial period in the development of the Trucial States, as the search for oil began, and while they were still very poor. He has written extensively about his enthusiasm for photography and the equipment he used, notably in the last chapter – entitled "al-'Akus", or "Reflections", as the local people charmingly called both the camera and the photographs – to each of the three *Arabian Albums* published in Dubai in the early 1990s.

Codrai's photography marked the arrival of modern techniques in the Trucial States: for example, although like Thesiger he preferred black-and-white, he was probably the first to try colour photography there when, in 1949, he was commissioned by the *National Geographic Magazine*. He was keen to update his equipment, graduating from a pre-War Cirroflex to a new Rolleiflex, and then to an Exakta, the first single-lens reflex 35mm camera. After Codrai, the deluge: many fine photographers came to the

Left Sir Rupert Hay in 1952 in the uniform of the Political Resident, Persian Gulf, a post he held first in 1941 and then from 1946 to 1953. On Codrai's principle that the best kind of camera is the one you have ready to hand, Hay was a keen exponent of the snapshot. The Box Brownie that he used had originally been designed by Frank Brownell, George Eastman's camera-maker. Eastman asked Brownell to design a very cheap and simple camera which could be used by anyone, even a child. The result was the famous Brownie, first introduced in 1900, and still popular in the 1950s.
Right Ronald Codrai poses for his own delayed-action exposure. With him are Shaikh Muhammad, father of the Ruler of Ras al-Khaimah Shaikh Saqr bin Muhammad, and Shaikh Humaid bin Muhammad, the Ruler's brother, on a visit to Dubai. (Codrai c.1949)

Trucial States for the oil companies in the 1950s and 1960s. They were the first professional photographers, and some of their work is represented here, since it vividly captures the old way of life. Just as significantly, the first cameras were acquired by local people. The first local professional photographer, 'Abd al-Karim Takizadeh, popularly known as "Captain", began taking group photographs at the beginning of the 1950s. In 1954 Codrai himself presented an early Polaroid (Lane's "One Minute Camera") to Shaikh Rashid of Dubai, and shortly afterwards Shaikh Saqr of Sharjah bought one.

In a telling opening to "Al-'Akus", Codrai noted: "Around the middle of this century a camera was still a rare sight in south-eastern Arabia and, when I photographed them, many of my subjects were seeing one for the first time. … Considering the extent to which people in the region had been isolated from such modern innovations, they were exceedingly tolerant of the strange object pointed in their direction."

Nor is Thesiger on record as having encountered local objections to being photographed. This was a very different response to that which was often encountered by early photographers in, for example, Saudi Arabia. There the objection was sometimes the traditional Islamic one to the creation of images of living things. More often it was the instinctive reaction of people unfamiliar with photography, but feeling that the lens pointing at them was an eye, perhaps an evil eye, and that,

in taking an image, the camera was making off with something vital that belonged to them.

Codrai's remark emphasises the obvious fact that, when he arrived on the Trucial Coast, the camera was a foreign eye, an instrument in the hands of foreign observers. Since Zwemer, photographs have been taken in the Trucial States for many different reasons, none of them in consultation with local people, who seldom saw the result. Significance is attached to the photograph initially by the photographer rather than by the subject of the picture. Subsequently, an image's significance is created by its viewers. When the photographer is alien to the culture into which he brings his camera, the significance he attaches to the picture may be very different from that which the subject might attach to it. When two cultures meet, one with a camera in hand, there is rich scope for distortion and misunderstanding of the resulting images. It is not surprising that, in extreme cases, photography has come to be seen not just as a kind of theft, a kind of expropriation of one culture by another, but also as a kind of misrepresentation which can only be malign. Idris, the young Algerian hero of Michel Tournier's novel *The Golden Droplet*, goes on a long, desperate search, which takes him as an immigrant to France, to recover a picture of himself taken by a French tourist. Eventually he realises the essential superficiality of images, and their deceptiveness as conveyors of meaning.

Even if taken with the greatest cultural empathy, a photograph freezes no more than a single moment in the flow of time, and thereby lends it an undue significance. This in itself is a misrepresentation of a kind, and is inevitable however much care is taken to diminish the moment's arbitrariness.

The photographs which have survived of the Trucial States can never deliver anything more than a chance, very partial picture of the old days. To yield up information about the past, they have to be used in conjunction with documentary evidence and what is known about the people and places that they show. There is today a new interest among the people of the Emirates in their past. At a basic level, photographs can act as a useful check on the tricks of time and memory. But if the greater value of a picture lies in the amount of information it carries and in the number of interpretations which can be placed upon it, then it is time for the people of the Emirates themselves to contribute their knowledge. This is especially urgent since so much is changing so rapidly, not only in their surroundings but in the people themselves, that the recent past will soon become a foreign country to the new generation. In responding to these pictures, the local people will greatly enhance the value of these photographs as historical records. In doing so they will also, in a sense, be re-possessing these images of their past.

THE PHOTOGRAPHS

Acknowledgements

Every effort has been made to trace and contact owners of copyright material. The authors and publisher gratefully acknowledge the following sources of photographs, with special thanks to The Abu Dhabi Company for Onshore Oil Operations (ADCO) and to British Petroleum. Thanks are due also to Ronald Codrai and Leslie McLoughlin, who made valuable comments on the photographs and text based on their personal knowledge of the area.

(l = left, r = right, t = top, b = bottom, c = centre)

The Abu Dhabi Company for Onshore Oil Operations (ADCO): dust jacket (front), 30-31, 31, 32*r*, 40-41, 43*t*, 49*b*, 50*l*, 50-51, 75, 77*tr*, 77*br*, 78*tl*, 82*b*, 83*t*, 83*b*, 84*t*, 84*b*, 85*t*, 85*b*, 88*bl*, 89, 116-117.

By courtesy of British Petroleum (BP Archive, University of Warwick, UK, and BP Photographic Library, London): 2-3, 4-5, 6, 32*t*, 32*b*, 33, 34, 35, 36*t*, 36*b*, 36-37, 39, 40*b*, 41*t*, 42, 43*b*, 44*t*, 44*l*, 44*r*, 45, 46, 47, 52, 53*b*, 53*tl*, 54*tl*, 54*tr*, 54*b*, 55*t*, 55*b*, 56, 57*t*, 57*b*, 58-59, 62*t*, 62*b*, 63, 64*l*, 64*r*, 65, 66, 67, 78*bl*, 86*t*.

Ronald Codrai: 1, 20*r*, 48, 81*r*, 82*t*, 100-101, 102-103, 104*tl*, 105, 119, 123*br*, 124, 125.

The Royal Geographical Society, London: dust jacket (back), 8, 13, 30*l*, 41*br*, 49*t*, 72*tl*, 72*b*, 72*tr*, 73, 96*t*, 96*b*, 99*b*, 103*rt*, 103*cr*, 104*tr*, 106*t*, 106*b*, 107*t*, 107*b*, 115*t*, 118*t*, 118-119, 122*t*, 122*b*, 123*t*, 123*bl*.

Maidstone Museum and Art Gallery, Maidstone Borough Council, UK: 10, 18.

Hermann Burchardt Collection, Museum für Volkerkunde, Berlin: 14*t*, 14*b*, 15*t*, 15*b*, 27, 28-29, 38*t*.

Gertrude Bell Photographic Archive, Department of Archaeology, University of Newcastle upon Tyne, UK: 12.

The British Library, Oriental and India Office Collections, London: 16.

The Historic Photographs Section, National Maritime Museum, London: 17*b*, 20*tr*, 90, 93*r*, 93*l*, 94, 95, 97*t*, 97*b*, 99*tr*, 111, 118*bl*.

Imperial War Museum, London: 19*t*.

Thomas Collection, Faculty of Oriental Studies Library, Cambridge University, UK: 19*br*, 20*tl*.

Kuwait Oil Company: 20*l*.

British Airways Archives, Hounslow, London: 20*bl*, 68, 70*t*, 70*b*, 71*t*, 71*b*, 98, 99*tl*, 104*b*, 108*t*, 108*b*, 109*t*, 109*b*, 110-111*t*, 110-111*b*, 112*t*, 112*b*, 113, 114, 120-121, 120*b*, 121.

©Wilfred Thesiger (Pitt Rivers Museum, Oxford and Curtis Brown on behalf of Wilfred Thesiger): 20*br*, 20*bc*, 38*b*, 40*t*, 53*tr*, 60, 61, 74, 76, 77*bl*, 77*tl*, 78-79, 80*tl*, 80*bl*, 80-81, 86*bl*, 86-87, 88*t*, 100*t*, 101*t*, 101*r*, 103*br*, 115*b*, 116*t*.

Sites of photographs in this work are annotated on this map
This map is not an authority on international boundaries

Strait of Hormuz

Khor al Sha'am

Tanbs

Ghubbat Ghazirah

O M A N

Sha'am

RUUS AL-JIBAL

Sirri

Rams

Gulf of Oman

Abu Musa

Ras Al-Khaimah
Jazirat al-Hamra

Dibah

Umm Al-Qaiwain

DHAHIRAH

Hamriyyah

'Ajman

Falaj al-Mu'alla

Masafi

Khor Fakkan

Sharjah

Wadi Ham

Dubai

Sir Bu Na'ir

Dhaid

Manamah

Khawanij

Milaihah

Bithnah

Fujairah

Das △

The Gulf

Jabal 'Ali

Kalba

Khor Kalba

Jabal Faqqah

BATINAH

Zirku

Shinas

Dalma

Mubarraz

Abu Dhabi •

Hatta

QATAR

Mahdhah

Ghaghah

Hili

Sir Bani Yas

Jabal Hafit

Buraimi

Abu al-Abyad

Al-'Ain

JABAL AKHDAR

Shuwaihat

Murban

BAINUNAH

O M A N

DHAFRAH

Dhank •

SAUDI ARABIA

U N I T E D   A R A B   E M I R A T E S

Asab

LIWA

Shah

Liwa Oases

Scale 0   50   100   200 kms

Umm al-Zamul

RUB' AL-KHALI

25

ABU DHABI

OF THE seven United Arab Emirates, Abu Dhabi is today by far the largest, occupying approximately 87% of the total land area. Its territory, with the exception of the oases of Liwa and al-'Ain, is the most arid of the Emirates: it is a desert which shelves gently into a long shoreline of shifting islands and salt flats *(sabkhahs)*, and then into a warm shallow sea. Its large territory indicates the extensive political influence built up in the past by the Al Bu Falah family (today the Al Nahyan) of the Bani Yas tribe, particularly during the reign of Shaikh Zayed bin Khalifah (r.1855-1909).

The people of Abu Dhabi were drawn from the desert tribal groups who grazed their herds in the Dhafrah and Bainunah areas on the northern fringe of the Rub' al-Khali. These tribespeople summered at the wells of Liwa, where some of them maintained palm groves. By the early 17th century they had coalesced into the dominant Bani Yas tribe. Their life began to change with the discovery, said to have been in 1761, of water on the uninhabited coast, on Abu Dhabi Island, which also had a sheltered anchorage.

With settlement on Abu Dhabi Island they greatly enlarged their resources: they became fishermen, pearlers and, soon, boat-builders and cargo traders. They even ferried their animals over to the larger islands to make use of the grazing. For they never abandoned their old way of life of herding and date cultivation: they simply combined it with their new maritime livelihoods. They developed a pattern of seasonal movement between coast, desert and oasis for at least part of each family unit – a pattern which is still a vivid memory today for many of the older generation. In this versatile lifestyle they showed themselves typical of the people of south-east Arabia, and distinct from the more specialised camel-herding tribes of inner Arabia north of the Rub' al-Khali.

The Bani Yas shared the grazing and wells of the Dhafrah and Bainunah with other tribes – the Al Murrah of al-Hasa, for example, and the Manasir, 'Awamir, Manahil and 'Afar – but the wells of the Liwa were more or less exclusive to them. During the 19th century the Bani Yas extended their dominance inland as far as the Al-'Ain region, where they developed some of the villages. The dominance of the Al Bu Falah family, not only within the Bani Yas but also over other tribes such as the Manasir, led to a process of centralised state formation which continued into the 20th century.

Opposite **The fort at Abu Dhabi, February 1904. (Burchardt)**

Shaikh Zayed bin Khalifah (shown leaning on the arm-rest, holding a camel-stick) conducting his *majlis* outside the fort at Abu Dhabi. Shaikh Zayed's long reign (1855-1909) established him as the most influential political figure on the Trucial Coast. Burchardt captioned this picture, curiously, as "Shaikh Ahmad bin Muhammad of Abu Dhabi in his *majlis*". He remarked that even the Shaikh's poorest subjects showed dignity without subservience, that the character of the government was patriarchal, and that in Abu Dhabi the life and property of the people were incomparably more secure than in Persia. The Shaikh's *majlis* lasted for two hours, after which all present enjoyed a good meal as his guests. (Burchardt 1904)

Below The interior of the Ruler's Palace at Abu Dhabi in the 1940s. By that time the old fort had been extended by the Ruler Shaikh Shakhbut bin Sultan. It is preserved today as the Documentation Centre of the Abu Dhabi Cultural Foundation. (R. Hay, 1941 or 1946-53)

Left An aerial view of Abu Dhabi in the 1940s shows the Ruler's Palace standing aloof from the town. Abu Dhabi suffered badly during the Second World War: starvation threatened, and many people emigrated to other Gulf states. Even by the late 1940s not much had improved. When Thesiger visited it in March 1948 he remarked on "the small, dilapidated town" of about two thousand people, stretching along the shore and dominated by its large castle. "Each morning the Shaikhs visited us, walking slowly across from the castle – Shakhbut, a stately figure in a black cloak, a little ahead of his brothers, followed by a throng of armed retainers."

Below The Palace at Abu Dhabi in 1949, as extended by Shaikh Shakhbut.

Left The Palace of the Ruler, Shaikh Shakhbut bin Sultan, in 1954.

Below The main gate and postern of the Palace, Abu Dhabi, in 1961.

Left A corner of Shaikh Shakhbut's Palace, Abu Dhabi, in 1954.

Right Even by 1962, when this aerial photograph was taken, the town of Abu Dhabi had hardly expanded despite the beginning of oil production in 1960.

Left The Ruler of Abu Dhabi, H.E. Shakhbut bin Sultan Al-Nahyan, at the entrance to his Palace in 1962.

Right The Palace, Abu Dhabi, in 1962.

One of Shaikh Shakhbut's falconers outside the Palace, Abu Dhabi, in 1957.

Below Horses were always a prized possession of Arabian rulers. These horses of Shaikh Shakhbut, seen here in Abu Dhabi in 1954, were a gift to him from the Ruler of Kuwait.

Members of Shaikh Shakhbut's
bodyguard mounted on horses given
by the Ruler of Kuwait, 1954.

The foreshore, Abu Dhabi, in February 1904, when the pearl fisheries were flourishing. Burchardt captioned this picture "Ships of the desert and sea". The vessel on the right with a fiddle-headed prow is a *battil*, while the pair in the centre with similar high-pointed sterns are large *baqqarahs*. Both types were ancient and were commonly used on the pearl banks. Abu Dhabi's was the largest of the trucial shaikhdoms' pearling fleets - in the early 1900s it numbered 410 boats – and so in those days the foreshore must have been crowded with vessels in the winter off-season. Burchardt noted the overwhelming importance of pearling to Abu Dhabi's economy, and commented that the coastal towns had grown into quite important trading centres as a result of the security at sea brought by the British. (Burchardt)

The Abu Dhabi shoreline in March 1948. The pearling boats would have gone with the collapse of the pearl trade in the 1920s. (Thesiger)

Coral stone for building is stacked along the shoreline at Abu Dhabi, 1954.

Wind swells the sails of a *jalibut* cruising among the Abu Dhabi islands. (Thesiger 1948)

Below Abu Dhabi Marine Areas Ltd (ADMA) used this large sailing *jalibut* for communications and transport in the early years of offshore oil exploration. (1954)

Local fishermen at Das Island make ready to place their wire lobster pots, with the first offshore rig *ADMA Enterprise* in the background during fitting out. (1958)

Below left Even by 1962 life had not changed much for Abu Dhabi's fishermen, although the occasional outboard motor made life easier for some, as on the boat in the background. The arrival of outboard motors spelled the end of the ancient double-ended type of craft like the small *baqqarah* in the foreground, as they could only be fitted to square sterns.

Below Local people and British naval officers during a visit to Dalma Island. Dalma had been an important centre for pearl divers and travelling pearl merchants during the heyday of the pearl trade. (R. Hay 1941 or 1946-53)

An Abu Dhabi blacksmith fashions a spatula for roasting coffee beans, while his daughter works the bellows. (1957)

Above Barasti wind-towers helped to ventilate the *suq*, Abu Dhabi. (November 1962)

Left A scene in the *suq* (market) in Abu Dhabi. (1957)

43

More scenes in the *suq*, Abu Dhabi, in 1962.

Typical *barasti* homesteads on the outskirts of Abu Dhabi in 1962. Such *barasti*s were the standard form of dwelling in the shaikhdoms before the arrival of prosperity. Made almost entirely from palm fronds, they were not only cool but surprisingly comfortable and private inside. Occasionally a *barasti* might even have a wind-tower made of palm fronds to catch the breeze.

Left The minaret of the Mosque, Abu Dhabi, in 1962.

Below As was customary in the settlements of Arabia, the Eid prayer at the end of Ramadan was attended by all the males of Abu Dhabi Town in the special Eid prayer enclosure outside the Palace. The open-air *mihrab* marking the *qiblah*, or direction of prayer, can be seen on the left of the picture. (March 1962)

The famous Maqta, or ford across the shallow strait dividing Abu Dhabi Island from the mainland, was always remarked upon by travellers. It could be crossed easily at low tide, and was guarded by a watchman in a tower which still survives.
(R. Hay 1941 or 1946-53)

Right In 1951 a causeway was built across the Maqta, greatly easing communication between Abu Dhabi Island and the mainland, and this police post was built to guard the crossing. (February 1961)

Left A tribesman leading a string of camels across the Maqta. They carry their own fodder, as animal feed was short on Abu Dhabi Island.
(Codrai c.1950)

49

An exploration rig at Well no. 1 at Shuwaihat in the west of Abu Dhabi territory. In October 1956 when this picture was taken, oil had not been discovered in commercial quantities.

Oil was first struck in commercial quantities in 1960 here at Murban Well no.3 in Abu Dhabi territory. (March 1960)

Above left Liwa villagers on the move from Asab to Shah oasis. Seasonal movements like this were a regular part of life. (March 1962)

Above Preparing a meal in good grazing country in Abu Dhabi's hinterland near Liwa. The tents of the bedouin in south-east Arabia were simpler, more rough-and-ready shelters than the black tents of the true nomadic bedouin tribes of Najd. (Thesiger 1949)

Left A family group on the move in the Liwa Oasis. Most Liwa families were semi-settled, owning palms in the Oasis but also having to support themselves by grazing camels in the winter months, or by pursuing other economic activities on the coast, usually fishing or pearling. (March 1962)

Previous page The Liwa Oasis comprises some four dozen tiny oases strung out along fifty miles or so among the sand dunes fringing the northern edge of the Rub' al-Khali. This settlement, Asab, situated in a hollow among the towering dunes, was typical.

Above A Liwa boy, already at home astride a camel. Unlike the bedouin tribesmen of central and northern Arabia, who sat on a large saddle-frame atop the hump, the tribespeople of the Emirates used the south Arabian type of camel saddle: a small saddle-frame in front of the hump, supporting a cushion allowing the rider to sit behind the hump, as shown here. (March 1962)

Above The scattered *barasti* enclosures of Shah village, Liwa. (March 1962)

A Liwa family outside their *barasti* house. (March 1962)

The mother grinds the coffee beans at Asab oasis, Liwa, among the scattered palms. (March 1962)

Serving coffee, Asab oasis. (March 1962)

The wells in the Liwa Oasis could support only a few
scattered date palms, not the regimented plantations of
Oman, Najd or Hasa Oasis. (March 1962)

Children in Asab oasis, Liwa.
(March 1962)

Left An elder of Liwa, named Rashid
bin Ghanim. (March 1962)

Overleaf A family on the move over
the dunes between the oasis villages,
Liwa. (1962)

57

Thesiger, in the late 1940s, enjoyed Shaikh Zayed's hospitality here at his fort at
Muwaiqih. (Thesiger 1949)

Shaikh Zayed bin Sultan Al-Nahyan with his falcon at Al-'Ain in 1950. In 1948 Shaikh Zayed became governor of the Al-'Ain region and was designated as successor to the Ruler. He subsequently became Ruler of Abu Dhabi in 1966. He has been President of the United Arab Emirates since the union was formed in 1971. (Thesiger)

Above Camel-riders assemble for a race, Al-'Ain. (March 1962)

Left Women prepare for a wedding party, Al-'Ain (March 1962)

Right A wedding dance at Al-'Ain. (March 1962)

Above Two scenes from Al-'Ain. (March 1962)

Right Eid ceremonies at the end of Ramadan, Al-'Ain. (March 1962)

Girls dancing during celebrations
marking the end of Ramadan at
Hili village. (March 1962)

His Highness Shaikh Zayed bin Sultan Al Nayhan leading dancers during the end of Ramadan ceremonies, Al-'Ain. (March 1962)

DUBAI

LIKE Abu Dhabi, Dubai is characterised chiefly by the desert and the sea, but also owns the enclave of Hatta in the mountains on the border with Oman. Being closer to the mountains of the Northern Emirates and Oman, Dubai's desert is less arid than Abu Dhabi's. It is low dune country which is relatively well vegetated, and areas of *ghaf* and acacia tree cover become more frequent.

As an Emirate, however, Dubai has been dominated by its chief town and port to an extent not found in the other Emirates. The town in fact grew up as three settlements – Shindaghah, Dubai and Deira – around the famous Creek, and today they have coalesced into a single city. Dubai's Creek is the finest natural harbour on the coast of the Emirates. Though silting has always been a problem, as it has for the creeks at Sharjah, Umm al-Qaiwain and other coastal towns, at Dubai it has been less serious, despite the shifting shoals at the Creek's entrance which were a hazard to seamen.

Shindaghah, on the sand-spit fronting the sea, was probably the first settlement – a fishing village mostly of Bani Yas tribesmen which, in the 18th century, was a dependency of Abu Dhabi. By 1820 there was a fort, the Fahidi Fort, in Dubai proper, where loading and unloading cargo was easier. But Dubai's rise was owed to the migration there in 1833 of the Al Bu Falasah section of the Bani Yas from Abu Dhabi. In those days Dubai Creek formed the boundary between the Bani Yas and Qasimi spheres of influence. From the beginning the ruling family, Al Maktum, strove to strengthen the role of Dubai, and during the 19th century Dubai began to eclipse Sharjah as a pearling and trading centre.

By 1900 Deira, the third quarter of town, had become the largest part of the town. Although Abu Dhabi had more pearling boats than any other shaikhdom, Dubai had the largest number of men employed on the pearl banks. Dubai as a whole expanded rapidly from the early 20th century, largely through the commercial astuteness of the ruling family who were, in effect, merchant princes. Trade was encouraged by abolishing import duty, and foreign traders – Indians and Persians – set up in business. The distinctive wind-tower style of building was first brought across the Gulf by Arabs fleeing from their homes on the Persian coast in the later 19th century, as the Persian government began to make life difficult for them.

Opposite Notables of Dubai in 1931.

This aerial view of Dubai in 1935 shows the three settlements which have, since the 1950s, grown together to make the modern city: Dubai (top), Shindaghah (right, fronting the sea), and Deira, the largest settlement jutting out into the Creek. (B.C.H. Cross)

A heavily laden *sambuq* gets under way in Dubai Creek, 1935. (B.C.H. Cross)

Above Shaikh Sa'id bin Maktum, Ruler of Dubai 1912-58, stands fourth from left in this picture taken in 1935. (B.C.H. Cross)

The Ruler of Dubai's falconers pose for the camera. (B.C.H. Cross 1935)

Nautical bustle in Dubai Creek.
(M. O'Connor c.1940)

Far right The *suq*, Dubai.
(R. Hay 1941 or 1946-53)

The waterfront, Dubai.
(R. Hay 1941 or 1946-53)

The customs house, Dubai. (R. Hay 1941 or 1946-53)

In Dubai *suq*, 1948. (Thesiger)

The palm frond shade structure lets through a
dappled sunlight in Dubai *suq*. (March 1960)

Wind-towers and *barasti*s, Dubai. Most people in Dubai lived in *barasti* compounds like the one in the foreground. More well-to-do people would build a house with a courtyard and wind-tower. Wind-towers were introduced by Arabs and Persians who emigrated to Dubai from the Persian coast in the late 19th century and after,

especially during the 1920s. Wind-towers were a special feature of the Bastakiyyah quarter of Dubai, immediately to the east of the Fahidi Fort. The piles of coral stone in the foreground of the picture have been delivered to site so that building can begin. The first house of concrete blocks was not built in Dubai till 1956. (Thesiger 1948)

Opposite, bottom left A corner of the Fahidi Fort, Dubai. The fort is now preserved as Dubai Museum. (Thesiger 1950)

Opposite, left Street and mosque in Dubai. (Thesiger 1950)

Opposite, right and bottom right Typical street scenes in Dubai. (March 1960)

Looking from Dubai towards Shindaghah on its sand-spit. Shindaghah was probably the oldest settlement on Dubai Creek, and in 1949 when this picture was taken was still separated from old Dubai by a space which flooded at high tide. The Ruler of Dubai traditionally lived in Shindaghah. Buri Khalifah, the old tower guarding Shindaghah, was said to be several centuries old. (Thesiger)

Opposite above left Close-up of a wind-tower, Dubai. The upper part consists of two diagonal cross-walls within the square structure. Wind from any quarter is caught and funnelled downwards into the living area below. Often a wet cloth was suspended horizontally across the base of the vent, to enhance the cooling effect. People would sit directly beneath the wind-tower to get the full benefit. (March 1960)

Opposite, below left Massed wind-towers on the waterfront, Dubai Creek. The recovery of Dubai's mercantile prosperity in the 1950s brought in its train an increase in wind-towers. (March 1962)

Left A landing-place for *abra*s, the small rowing boats which used to ferry people across the Creek from Dubai to Deira – and still do today. (Thesiger 1949)

Below left A newly painted dhow on the Creek waterfront. (Thesiger 1949)

Right A *ghanjah* or *kutiyyah* under full sail off Dubai. (Codrai c.1950)

Below The stern of a large *baghlah* or *ghanjah* drawn up on shore for re-caulking. (Thesiger 1948)

A pearling boat heading back into Dubai. When this picture was taken pearling was no longer an important economic activity. Before the First World War Dubai sent 335 boats to the pearl banks, as compared with 410 from Abu Dhabi, 360 from Sharjah, Khan, Hamriyyah, Hirah and Ras al-Khaimah, 70 from Umm al-Qaiwain and 40 from 'Ajman. In all, more than 22,000 men from the Trucial Coast went to the pearl banks every summer during the heyday of the pearl trade before the 1920s. (Codrai 1949)

Dubai Creek in October 1956.

Left and below Dubai Creek in October 1956.

Dubai Creek in March 1958. Dubai's population stood at around 40,000 at that time.

The first step in building a boat was to lay the keel, shown here in a Dubai boatyard in front of a new vessel. Then the stem- and stern-posts were added. Next the hull planking would be bent into shape and fitted with joints butted carefully together. Ribs were added after the hull planking, and everything was then clenched together with iron nails. The entire process was done by eye, without drawings. Wood was imported from India. (June 1959)

Launching a newly built *jalibut*,
Dubai. (June 1959)

A *kutiyyah* from India in Dubai.
*Kutiyyah*s were basically the same as
*ghanjah*s – square-sterned with a
carved poop, like small *baghlah*s – and
both were common cargo vessels.

Left A *boum* lies at anchor in the Creek. The double-ended *boum*, with its distinctive stem-post, was especially associated with Kuwait and was the main cargo-carrier of the Gulf. (March 1962)

Below A small fishing *baqqarah* at Dubai. The typical high pointed stern of the *baqqarah* and *battil* was designed for the attachment of a deep, rope-operated rudder, which had to be unshipped when the boat was in shallow water or beached. This type of craft is very ancient, dating back at least to the 12th-13th centuries, when they were stitched rather than nailed together. (Thesiger 1950)

Preparing to go fishing on the beach off
Shindaghah, Dubai. (Thesiger 1950)

Fishermen dry their nets on the beach. The water barrel was an essential part of every boat's equipment. (Thesiger 1950)

Dubai fishermen examine a catch of fish. (February 1959)

Shaikh Rashid bin Saʻid Al-Maktum, Ruler of Dubai, in 1960. He ruled Dubai from 1958 till his death in 1990. From 1971 until his death he was the first Vice-President of the United Arab Emirates.

SHARJAH, RAS AL-KHAIMAH AND THE NORTHERN EMIRATES

ALL THE northern Emirates today share in common a background as part of the Qasimi domain in the late 18th and 19th centuries. Unlike the Bani Yas of Abu Dhabi and Liwa, the Qawasim were a small clan which succeeded in uniting a large number of coastal and inland Arab tribes including those of Qishm and Lingah on the Persian coast.

Their leadership outlasted the suppression of their maritime power by the British in 1820, and was recognised in the mid-19th century over the entire area north of a line between Sharjah and Khor Kalba on the Shimailiyyah coast (with the exception of the inaccessible Ruus al-Jibal north of Dibah and Sha'am). This historical dominance is reflected today in the patchwork of territories which still make up the Emirates of Sharjah and Ras al-Khaimah, the two chief centres of the Qawasim.

For most of the 19th century Sharjah was the most populous port on the Trucial Coast. Sharjah, Ras al-Khaimah, Hamriyyah, Hirah and Khan together provided more boats than Dubai to the pearl banks, but not as many as Abu Dhabi. Most of these came from Sharjah, which was the chief trading centre of the coast until eclipsed by Dubai.

The creeks at Sharjah and Ras al-Khaimah suffered more than Dubai's from the north-south current along the coast which has silted up their entrances. The smaller Emirates of 'Ajman and Umm al-Qaiwain occupy very similar positions, on sand-spits fronting inland lagoons. In the case of Umm al-Qaiwain this appears to be the relic of an ancient wadi delta, which in antiquity was the site of important settlements.

The spit on which the town of Ras al-Khaimah was situated fronts a deeper inlet forming a natural dhow port. The area has a long history, reaching back to the mediaeval port of Julfar and further, to pre-Islamic times. Ras al-Khaimah is close to the northern end of the narrowing plain between the mountains and the Gulf, and its inland possessions include rugged mountain areas as well as the fertile, relatively well-watered coastal strip. Here its palm groves and agriculture were far more abundant than those of any other shaikhdom.

The people of Ras al-Khaimah's territory shared the versatility typical of many tribal groups in south-east Arabia. In the early part of this century, the purely nomadic way of life accounted for only about

Opposite Arab shaikhs and bodyguards on board *HMS Hardinge* in 1903, during Lord Curzon's visit to Sharjah. By this time several different types of snapshot cameras were available which, depending on the model, could produce negatives of 1⅞ x 2½ inches up to 3¼ x 5½ inches in size.

one-tenth of the population. Many people would take part in two economic activities during the course of a year: goat- or camel-herdsmen might also own date palms; mountain cultivators might spend the summer on the pearl banks; a herdsman might spend the winter in the desert and the summer fishing; or a sailor might help with the date harvest between trading voyages. Most marked was the seasonal migration between the mountains and the coast.

Fujairah is the only Emirate to be confined exclusively to the Arabian Sea coast of the UAE. Traditionally it was the centre of the most influential tribe of the Shimailiyyah coast and mountains, the Sharqiyin. Fujairah declared its independence of Qasimi rule in 1901, whereas Kalba, Khor Fakkan and part of Dibah remain to this day within Sharjah territory. The economy of this coast depended on cultivation and fishing, and never depended on pearling to the same extent as on the Gulf side.

Internal boundaries in the Northern Emirates

Source: Heard-Bey, F. *From Trucial states to United Arab Emirates* 1982

Above Sharjah Creek in c.1907-9. (A.N. Gouldsmith)

On Sharjah waterfront, c.1907-9. (A.N. Gouldsmith)

Opposite Sharjah Fort, 1907-9. (A. N. Gouldsmith)

An armed dhow at Sharjah in 1920 – a snapshot by a naval man. By 1920 several manufacturers were producing small-format roll film cameras, which became more and more popular. The best-seller was the Vest Pocket Kodak which sold in great numbers between 1912 and 1926, closely followed by the No.0 Brownie which took Vest Pocket-size film. The Ensign box and folding cameras were made in four sizes by the British firm of Houghton's Ltd. (R. Goldrich)

Views of Sharjah Creek in 1926: two interesting snapshot views. The early cheap cameras before 1926 were unsatisfactory for close-ups, as they had fixed-focus lenses effective only at a distance of two metres or more.
(A. T. Wilson)

A common type of small fishing
boat, seen here at Sharjah, was the
shashah, made from the mid-ribs of
date palm fronds. The high standard
of these pictures suggests that
Vaughan's camera was of a better
quality than most naval men's snapshot cameras. (H.R. Vaughan 1929)

Sharjah and its Creek in 1935. The
Creek with its long, narrow outlet to
the sea was vulnerable to silting up.
When this picture was taken, Sharjah
was newly prosperous, since the
Trucial Coast's airfield for Imperial
Airways was located there in 1932.
The settlement on the sea front is
Hirah. (B.C.H. Cross)

Opposite left Shaikh Sultan bin Saqr
Al-Qasimi, Ruler of Sharjah 1924-51,
with Colonel G. Loch in 1935. Loch
was British Political Agent at Bahrain
from 1933 to 1937 and responsible,
through the Residency Agent, for the
affairs of the Trucial Coast.
(B.C.H. Cross)

Opposite bottom The British Political
Agency at Sharjah. A full-time British
Political Officer was first appointed to
Sharjah in 1949. In 1953 the post was
raised to that of Political Agent, and in
1954 the Political Agency was moved to
Dubai, reflecting its growing importance.
(R. Hay 1948-53)

Right 'Isa bin 'Abd al-Latif, seen here in c.1929, was Britain's Residency Agent at Sharjah for the whole Trucial Coast, from 1919 to 1935. Between them 'Isa, his father and grandfather had served as Residency Agents at Sharjah since 1866, and wielded immense influence on the Coast. Himself a wealthy merchant with interests in Dubai, 'Isa imported the first motor car into the shaikhdoms in 1928. The post of Residency Agent was abolished in 1949.
(H. R. Vaughan)

Right and opposite Sharjah Creek and waterfront in 1948. (Thesiger)

Below Sharjah Town from the landward side, showing the typical assemblage of *barasti* houses and wind-towers. The circular wind-tower on the left was the only one of its type in the Trucial States. (Codrai 1951)

Below The *suq* at
Sharjah in 1948.
(Thesiger)

The Fort at Sharjah with its unusual tower in 1951. The flag at half-mast marks the passing of the Ruler Shaikh Sultan bin Saqr. (Codrai)

Right Mining for red oxide on Abu Musa Island. Red oxide used to be in demand abroad as a pigment before the introduction of chemical paints. (R. Hay 1941 or 1946-53)

Right Dhaid lies inland in Sharjah territory. Like other agricultural centres in the Dhahirah, it depended on a *falaj* from the mountains. One of the irrigation channels is seen here. (R. Hay 1941 or 1946-53)

Below Bedouin water their camels from a well between Al-'Ain and Sharjah. (Thesiger 1948)

Goatherds water their flocks at a well in the northern Emirates. (Codrai 1953)

Khor Fakkan. (R. Hay 1941 or 1946-53)

Khor Fakkan, seen here in 1935, was one of Sharjah's important dependencies, with Kalba and part of Dibah, on the east or Shimailiyyah coast of the shaikhdoms. (B.C.H. Cross)

Opposite The Shaikh's fort at Kalba in 1951. Kalba, which was traditionally part of the Qasimi shaikhdom of Sharjah, was recognised by Britain as independent in 1936 to encourage its Shaikh to grant landing rights for aircraft. In 1951 Kalba reverted to Sharjah. (Codrai 1951)

Outside the fort at Ras al-Khaimah in 1905, on the morning that Cox prepared for his second journey into the interior of the shaikhdoms. "We experienced no difficulty in obtaining camels at Ras al-Khaimah," wrote Cox, "and only spent one night there, leaving our quarters in the Shaikh's fort the next forenoon in the presence of an interested crowd." (P.Z. Cox)

Below An agricultural village with its date plantation on the mainland of Ras al-Khaimah in 1926. The narrowing coastal plain was relatively well-watered owing to its proximity to the mountains. (A.T.Wilson)

Barasti enclosures and palm groves on the mainland of Ras al-Khaimah in 1925-6. (G.M. Lees)

Below The town of Ras al-Khaimah occupied an easily defended sand-spit enclosing a lagoon which was well protected from the weather. (A.T. Wilson 1926)

The town of Ras al-Khaimah, its
sand-spit and lagoon in an aerial
photograph of 1935. (RAF)

A panoramic view of the town
looking north.
(B.C.H. Cross 1935 or before)

Looking north-east over the outskirts
of Ras al-Khaimah towards the lagoon.
(B.C.H. Cross 1935 or before)

Below A view of the foreshore within
the lagoon, looking west.
(B.C.H. Cross 1935 or before)

The beach and anchorage of Ras al-Khaimah within the lagoon. This and the next picture were taken with a panoramic camera. The principle of a rotating-lens panoramic camera was an old one: daguerrotypes had been taken by this method in the 1840s. In the early 1860s panoramic wet-plate cameras were produced which incorporated a spring motor to rotate the entire camera on a platform. By 1900 the panoramic principle was available even with a snapshot camera via the Panoram Kodak. Such devices tended to appeal only to the professional or real enthusiast, however. (B.C.H. Cross 1935 or before)

A *jalibut* under sail in the lagoon, Ras al-Khaimah, taken with a panoramic camera. (B.C.H. Cross 1935 or before)

Far right A large cargo *baqqarah* gets underway off Ras al-Khaimah. (H.R. Vaughan September 1928)

III

British Air Ministry surveyors placing marked posts in order to locate soundings for cross-sections of the lagoon, Ras al-Khaimah. Ras al-Khaimah was first identified in 1929 as a suitable place for flying boats to land and refuel. The motor boat belonged to the Shaikh of Sharjah whose flag can be seen at the stern. (B.C.H. Cross, 1935 or before)

A refuelling dhow in the lagoon, Ras al-Khaimah, for the RAF flying boat squadron. This was placed here in 1930 against local opposition. One of the RAF's tasks was to protect the civilian air route which was then being established between Iraq and India. When Sharjah granted a landing ground in 1932, the route via the Trucial Coast was established for both flying boats and normal aircraft. The taller building in the background was known as "Isa's House". (B.C.H. Cross 1935 or before)

Shaikh Muhammad bin Salim (centre), brother of the Ruler of Ras al-Khaimah Shaikh Sultan bin Salim, poses for the camera with his young son. (B.C.H. Cross, 1935 or before)

Left One of Ras al-Khaimah's watchtowers. Typically, these watchtowers had no entrance at ground level: one had to climb up a rope to one of the lower apertures. (B.C.H. Cross 1935 or before)

Right The Ruler's fort at Ras al-Khaimah. (R. Hay 1941 or 1946-53)

Right The Ruler's fort at Ras al-Khaimah. (Thesiger 1950)

The market at Ras al-Khaimah. (Thesiger 1950)

Fishing boats in the creek, Ras al-Khaimah.
(March 1958)

The watchtower at Rams, a small shaikhdom to the north of Ras al-Khaimah, of which it was traditionally a dependency. (R. Hay 1941 or 1946-53)

An unidentified group at 'Ajman, c.1907-9. (A.N. Gouldsmith)

'Ajman and the Ruler's fort, showing the mix of palms, *barasti* houses and more substantial dwellings which typified settled life on the coast in the old days. (Codrai c.1950)

Below The Ruler of 'Ajman, Shaikh Rashid bin Humaid, with his camel. Shaikh Rashid ruled from 1928 to 1981. The ruling family of 'Ajman belongs to the Al Bu Kharaiban section of the Na'im, the important inland tribe which dominated the Buraimi Oasis and formed an important part of the inhabitants of Sharjah and of Sharjah's inland dependency of Dhaid. The ruling families of nearby Hirah and Hamriyyah, both dependencies of Sharjah, came from the Darawishah sub-section of the Na'im. (R. Hay 1941 or 1946-53)

A panorama of Umm al-Qaiwain.
(B.C.H. Cross 1935 or before)

Like other coastal towns, Umm
al-Qaiwain was situated on a sand-
spit which separated a protected
anchorage from the sea. Umm
al-Qaiwain's lagoons are among the
most extensive on the Arabian coast
of the Gulf, and its mangrove
thickets, sea-grass beds and mud-flats
provided an important food resource
for marine life and people. This aerial
picture was taken in 1935. (RAF)

The Residency Agent 'Isa bin 'Abd al-Latif (second from right) with some of the notables of Umm al-Qaiwain in 1931. Unlike the other northern shaikhdoms on the Gulf coast, the people of Umm al-Qaiwain belonged to a single tribe, the Al 'Ali, who also inhabited the inland oasis nearby of Falaj Al-Mu'alla. A bedouin group living along the coast towards Jazirat al-Hamra completed the spectrum of seafarers, fishermen, pearlers, cultivators and herdsmen who made up this typically versatile tribe.

The Ruler of Umm al-Qaiwain, Shaikh Ahmad bin Rashid Al-Mu'alla, hosts an official visit. (R. Hay 1941 or 1946-53)

Below The impressive fort at Umm al-Qaiwain still stands to this day. (R. Hay 1941 or 1946-53)

Above Fujairah was dominated by its imposing fort.
(R.Hay 1941 or 1946-53)

Left The Ruler of Fujairah, Shaikh Muhammad bin Hamad Al-Sharqi, who ruled from 1932 to 1974.
(R. Hay 1941 or 1946-53)

Right Shaikh Muhammad bin Hamad with some of his people at Fujairah. Like Umm al-Qaiwain, Fujairah was basically a one-tribe settlement, whose people belonged to the Sharqiyyin, the chief tribe of the Shimailiyyah coast.
(Codrai 1950)

Fujairah, though a coastal settlement, was built somewhat inland.
It dominated the Wadi Ham, one of the main passes across the
Shimailiyyah mountains from the northern Dhahirah, where it
opens onto the coastal plain. (Codrai 1950)

A typical well used by villagers in the mountainous
hinterland of Fujairah. (Codrai 1951)

BIBLIOGRAPHY

ABBREVIATION
GJ   *The Geographical Journal.* London.

ABDULLAH, Muhammad Morsy, *The United Arab Emirates. A Modern History.* London 1994.

ANTHONY, T.A. "Documentation of the Modern History of Bahrain from American Sources (1900-1938)", *Bahrain Through the Ages: The History,* ed. A.K. Khalifah and M. Rice. London 1993.

BIDWELL, R., (ed.), *The Affairs of Kuwait 1896-1905.* Cambridge 1965.

BIDWELL, Robin, *Travellers in Arabia.* London 1976

BURCHARDT, H. "Ost-Arabien von Basra bis Maskat auf Grund eigener Reisen", *Zeitschrift der Gesellschaft für Erdkunde zu Berlin,* Berlin 1906.

ÇIZGEN, E. *Photography in the Ottoman Empire.* Istanbul 1987.

CODRAI, R. *The Seven Shaikhdoms.* London 1990. *Abu Dhabi. An Arabian Album.* Dubai 1992. *Dubai. An Arabian Album.* Dubai 1992. *The North-East Shaikhdoms. An Arabian Album.* Dubai 1993. *One Second in the Arab World.* Dubai 1995.

COE, B.W. "The Evolution of Photography", *The British Journal of Photography,* 12th May. London 1972.

COE, B. and GATES, P. *The Snapshot Photographers: The Rise of Popular Photography 1888-1939.* London 1977.

COTTRELL, A.J. (ed), *The Persian Gulf States.* Baltimore 1980.

COX, P.Z. "Some Excursions in Oman", *GJ* LXVI no.3, September 1925.

CURSETJEE, C.M. *A Voyage in the Gulf: C.M. Cursetjee's* The Land of the Date, 1918. Ed. Paul Rich. Cambridge 1991.

CURZON, G.N. *Persia and the Persian Question.* London 1892.

DIXEY, A.D. "In the Persian Gulf", *Church Missionary Review* 58. London 1907.

FACEY, W.H.D. and GRANT G. *Saudi Arabia by the First Photographers.* London 1996.

GOLDSMID, F.J. *Telegraph and Travel.* London 1874.

GRAHAM-BROWN, S. *Images of Women: The Portrayal of Women in Photography of the Middle East, 1860-1950.* London 1988.

GRANT, Gillian, (ed.) *Historical Photographs of the Middle East from the Middle East Centre, St Antony's College, Oxford.* Leiden 1985.

GRANT, Gillian, *Middle Eastern Photographic Collections in the United Kingdom.* Middle East Libraries Committee Research Guides 3, Durham 1989.

GRAVES, P. *The Life of Major-General Sir Percy Cox.* London.

GREAT BRITAIN, Admiralty, Naval Intelligence Division. *Iraq and the Persian Gulf.* London 1944.

GUILLAIN, C. *Documents sur l'histoire, la géographie et le commerce de l'Afrique orientale.* 2 vols. and Atlas. Paris 1856.

HARRISON, P.W. *The Arab at Home.* London 1924.

HAY, R. *The Persian Gulf States.* Washington 1959.

HEARD-BEY, F. *From Trucial States to United Arab Emirates.* Harlow 1982.

HENDERSON, E. *This Strange Eventful History.* London.

HOGARTH, D.G. *The Penetration of Arabia.* London 1904.

HUNTER, F.F. "Reminiscences of the Map of Arabia and the Persian Gulf", *GJ* LIV, pp.353-363. London 1919.

JEFFREY, I. *Photography. A Concise History.* London 1981.

JOUANNIN, A. "Sur les rives du Golfe Persique. Notes de voyage 1903", *Bulletin de la Société de Géographie Commerciale de Paris* 26. Paris 1904.

KELLY, J.B. *Britain and the Persian Gulf 1795-1880.* London 1968. "A Prevalence of Furies: Tribes, Politics and Religion in Oman and Trucial Oman", in *The Arabian Peninsula: Society and Politics,* ed. D. Hopwood. London 1972. *Arabia, the Gulf and the West.* London 1980.

KUMAR, R. *India and the Persian Gulf Region, 1858-1907.* London 1965.

KUNZ, G.F. and STEVENSON, C.U. *The Book of the Pearl. History, Art, Science and Industry of the Queen of the Gem.*

LORIMER, J.G. *Gazetteer of the Persian Gulf, 'Oman and Central Arabia.* 2 vols. Calcutta.

McLOUGHLIN, L.J. *Ibn Saud. Founder of a Kingdom.* London 1993.

MILES, S.B. *The Countries and Tribes of the Persian Gulf.* 2nd edition, London 1966.

OPPENHEIM, M. von, *Vom Mittelmeer zum persischen Golf, durch der Hauran, die Syrische Wüste und Mesopotamien.* Berlin 1899-1900.

PALGRAVE, W.G. *Narrative of a Year's Journey Through Central and Eastern Arabia (1862-3).* 2 vols., London.

PEREZ, N. *Focus East: Early Photography in the Near East (1839-1885).* New York 1988.

PIRENNE, J. *À la découverte de l'Arabie.* Paris 1958.

AL-QASIMI, Dr Sultan ibn Muhammad, *The Myth of Arab Piracy in the Gulf.* London 1986.

REZVAN, E. *Russian Ships in the Gulf, 1899-1903.* Guildford 1993.

SAID ZAHLAN, R. *Origins of the United Arab Emirates. A Political and Social History of the Trucial States.* London 1978.

THESIGER, W. "Desert Borderlands of Oman", *GJ* CXVI, 1950. *Arabian Sands.* London 1959. *Desert, Marsh and Mountain. The World of a Nomad.* London 1979. *Visions of a Nomad.* London 1987. *The Thesiger Collection.* Dubai 1991. *Wilfred Thesiger's Photographs,* "A Most Treasured Possession". Pitt Rivers Museum Catalogue introduced by E. Edwards. Oxford 1993.

THOMAS, Bertram, *Alarms and Excursions in Arabia.* London 1931. *Arabia Felix.* London 1932.

TIDRICK, K. *Heart-beguiling Araby. The English Romance with Arabia.* Cambridge 1981.

TOURNIER, M. *The Golden Droplet.* London 1988. (First published as *La goutte d'or*).

TRENCH, R. *Arabian Travellers.* London 1986.

TUSON, P. *The Records of the British Residency and Agencies in the Persian Gulf.* India Office Library and Records, London 1979.

VACZEK, L. and BUCKLAND, G. *Travellers in Ancient Lands: A Portrait of the Middle East, 1839-1919.* Boston 1981.

WHIGHAM, H.J. *The Persian Problem.* London 1903.

WILSON, A.T. *The Persian Gulf.* London 1928.

WINDER, R. Bayly, *Saudi Arabia in the Nineteenth Century.* London 1965.

WINSTONE, H.V.F. *The Illicit Adventure.* London 1982.

WINSTONE, H.V.F. and FREETH, Z. *Explorers in Arabia.* London 1978.

ZWEMER, S.M. *Arabia: the Cradle of Islam.* New York 1900. "Three Journeys in Northern Oman", *GJ* XIX no. 1, January 1902.

INDEX

Page numbers in bold refer to the photographs